MAGIC AND MYSTICS OF JAVA

By the same Author

MAGIC AND MYSTICS
OF JAVA

by

NINA EPTON

THE OCTAGON PRESS
LONDON

SBN: 900860 39 1

Printed in Great Britain by Tonbridge Printers Ltd.,
Tonbridge, Kent.

FOR
MAHIR,
ATIKA, AND ADILA

PART I

JAVA, LAND OF THE MOONLIGHT ORCHID

CONTENTS

Contents

PART IV: MAGIC AND MYSTICS OF JAVA

THE EIGHT-THOUSAND-MILE FLIGHT TO JAVA

IN the dusk at London Airport the silver Skymaster waited. A straggling line of fifty passengers walked up the steps and disappeared inside to be taken in charge by a stewardess who packed us away as neatly as eggs in the creature's wide, warm flanks.

At eleven o'clock at night, we touched down at Frankfort-on-Main in Germany. Frankfort was bleak, the straw-haired frauleins disinterested, and everything we could have spent our money on was firmly closed down for the night. We glared at each other in a draughty waiting-room feeling like hospital patients whose beds were being remade in the wards.

We were marched out again at three in the morning, but this was now Rome. Our drowsiness left us and we found ourselves thawing and smiling back, first a little wanly then with more assurance, in response to the beaming faces and flashing eyes of the Italians on the restaurant terrace. Large parties of people had driven up to the airport for the sole purpose of enjoying themselves. To them this was just another café, a little different from those in town because of the arrivals from the sky that periodically disgorge odd groups of human beings like us. We provided entertainment and people leaned back in their chairs as we passed to guess where we came from and what we could be in ordinary life. The airport was gay with lights, sparkling glass, and darting waiters who entered into the fun with zest.

After more refreshments (we never stopped eating and drinking) we looked up, surprised to find that most of the people had mysteriously melted away and that we were enveloped in a rosy haze. The other members of our group had become transfigured: drawn, enigmatic, and ethereal, like convalescents. Then we began to distinguish hills in the distance and the ashen-grey silhouette

of silent church towers. Dawn had come with magical swiftness
and had taken us completely unawares.

From southern Italy's barren toe we sped over the rocky island
birthplaces of great Greek tragedies and caught a brief glimpse of
the imperious Acropolis dominating Athens and the bay of
Corinth. I remembered reading how an American lady of eighty-
two had crossed the Atlantic just to see the Acropolis by moonlight; it was the last thing she wanted to see before she died. Even
in the sunlight it was worth travelling many miles to see.

Beyond this classical frontier which was still part of our Western
world lay a red tumult of deserts and shark-infested coasts. The
sun looked fiery enough to crack the porcelain-fragile sky from
top to bottom. It had already sucked up all the water from the
snake-like depressions that once were rivers. Every trace of life-
giving green had been scorched off long ago. The gaping earth
was as brown as an overdone pie-crust.

A ridge of crimson mountains near the sea grew gradually more
distinct as we nosed down smoothly towards Beyrouth. 'We
shall be stopping here for just over an hour. Light refreshments
will be served at the airport,' chanted the Australian air hostess in
coolly impartial tones.

The airport was a huge contemporary building designed to
impress tourists but with no thought for weary travellers. We
were walked by an impassive Lebanese air hostess through endless corridors and up wide marble steps to a restaurant filled with
empty tables that stretched in sepulchral white rows. On our
listless way, we passed an alley of posters advertising world-
famous airlines, but there was also a small newcomer among
them, its presence indicative of the new desert prosperity based
upon oil: this was the Kuwait airline, ready to carry anybody
who cared to see what the multi-millionaire Sheik of Kuwait is
doing with his fabulous royalties. I hoped that he had been plant-
ing trees in his arid sector of the Persian Gulf. Here in Lebanon
we were still within sight of vegetation; even from the airport
we could smell the biblical cedars.

On our way back to the aeroplane from our 'light refreshments'

we caught up with a band of Arabs who looked as if they were
bound for a distant oasis thick with date-palms and tinkling with
streams. They were dressed for a camel-ride rather than an aeroplane journey and they swished past us in wide black woollen
cloaks, totally absorbed by their bulky bundles (some of these
were wives) and numerous babies. The men carried luggage
upon their heads; they were family men and we saw that most of
them even knew how to deal with the distressing accidents that
befall infants at the most inopportune moments. 'What an efficient father!' exclaimed an English woman traveller as a young
Arab held his babe's feet in one hand while his wife—who was
hampered by her heavy black veil—struggled to change its
nappie. Both father and mother passed a minute pair of rub-
berized knickers between its legs; the woman wrapped the baby
in a pink shawl, her husband rolled up the tiny mattress after
tucking pillow and rugs inside, lifted it to his head and stalked
out to the waiting plane; his plump wife followed, quivering like
a jelly-fish and almost as shapeless.

A meek but modern Lebanese lady and her two small children,
chaperoned by her young brother, joined our party at Beyrouth
and flew with us all the way to Djakarta in the most unsuitable
clothes. The mother, whose short hair was set according to the
latest Parisian fashion (France may be turned out of her overseas
territories, but never the products of Paris which, like Bismarck's
stomach, are international), wore a black lamé costume, while
her sad-faced but uncomplaining children were encased in woollen
slacks and coats. And we stopped at places where the temperature was well over a hundred degrees!

The barren parapets of the Persian Gulf were soon left behind
and before we realized where we were, the 'plane was diving
down to the twinkling lights of Karachi. Before one is allowed
to alight in the capital of Pakistan, fiercely moustached individuals with raised eyes and arms holding 'flit' sprayers walk up
and down the plane to disinfect travellers. This performance
could be delightful . . . if only we had been sprayed with Eastern
perfume. What a pleasant introduction it would have been to

this exotic land! Instead, we reached for our handkerchiefs, sneezed violently, and felt aggressive. Most of the airport employees looked aggressive too. Perhaps it was because of their whiskers and their magnificent moustaches coaxed to such a fine, swordlike point.

Tired European food was served in the resthouse restaurant by splendid lion-waisted waiters in white trousers and tunics, navy-blue cummerbunds, and arrogant turbans draped with individual fantasy, as if they had just been taking part in a turban-setting contest. Only a warlike race could have devised such turbans. Advance, cohorts of elephants! Blow, silver trumpets! On with the drummers! The owners of such princely turbans were never intended to humble themselves by carrying fish mornay for jaded travellers such as us.

The unceasing whirr of the engines prevented me from sleeping as we crossed the entire breadth of India during the night. The entire breadth of India with its teeming millions, its jungle animals and its great rivers—dreaming, hunting, rolling in the immense blackness beneath us. At dawn, we were casually and prosaically informed that we were approaching Calcutta where more 'light refreshments' would be served.

We left the aircraft again in the steamy, stifling atmosphere of a Somerset Maugham novel and were led into a flimsy, low-roofed building—mud-coloured to match the landscape. Vultures with brooding eyes flapped awkwardly along the gutters, looking at us sideways. We may have *felt* half dead but the mere sight of these necrophil birds made us brace ourselves up instinctively. After gazing at us mournfully they hopped off elsewhere like rapacious undertakers.

An Indian woman in an orange sari, lean as an advertisement in aid of a famine relief fund, squatted by the powder-room and shook her head resignedly when we complained about the plumbing deficiencies. Three-quarters of the globe seem to lack efficient plumbers. What splendid scope there is for them! Be a plumber and see the world!

A few hours later—only another eight hundred miles east—

16

we lunched in Bangkok, where the electric fans had ceased to function and nobody had the energy to make them work again. Shaven-headed Buddhist monks stood and watched us from a distance, only a little more kindly than Calcutta's vultures. They were probably pitying us for our restlessness within the Wheel of Life. Here too we saw the names of more unfamiliar airlines, inviting us to visit Vietnam and Vietmin in Indo-China.

Sultry Siamese air hostesses swayed past us, shaking their thick black hair over sensitive shoulders with sidelong glances that made our male passengers regret we were only staying in Bangkok for lunch. They were very different from *our* breezy, nurse-like air hostesses.

The Chinese girls in Singapore had almost as much sex appeal but their eyes were keener and more calculating. They were not secretive about their figures and obviously wore nothing but a brassiere and a suspender-belt under their skin-tight Chinese dresses, topped by a stiff round collar of an almost military cut; the provocatively slit skirt, however, revealed slim nylon-stockinged legs up to mid-thigh level.

We were carefully sorted out at Singapore where transit passengers were handed a folder of typed instructions giving a room number in a hotel and the time at which we would be called next morning for the last stage of the journey. The mere thought of a whole night in a real bed was exhilarating, even when I was told that I would have to share my room with a matronly missionary on her way to convert the ex-head-hunters of New Guinea to our way of life.

There is nothing I find likeable about Singapore except for its Eastern smells. These do not please everybody, I know. Singapore reeks of fried rice, sweet wood-smoke, and the spicy sweat of golden bodies.

Those parts of the town built by the British bear the hallmark of the City of London. Imagine the corner of London occupied by the Bank and the Mansion House surrounded by streets of tightly packed, one-storeyed shops displaying Chinese signs and you have a good idea of what the centre of Singapore is like.

British merchants, Chinese merchants, and before them, Arab merchants, struggled for supremacy here. The place was doomed from the start. Like most strategically important places, it lacks poetry.

We were warned that there was 'a certain amount of unrest' in Singapore at that moment; the usual coach tour of the city by night had been cancelled and we were advised not to wander far from our hotel. But Raffles Hotel, with its lofty, air-conditioned rooms and troops of soft-footed Malayan servants, gave us a perfect illusion of peace, luxury, and security. The food was excellent, especially an Eastern fish course romantically baptized: 'Kontiki kuroa'.

There was a disturbing diversion in the middle of the night, however, when our bedroom door opened suddenly and a man unsteadily groped his way in. I woke with a start and sat up in bed, rubbing my eyes. Could it be six o'clock already and was this the Malayan servant come to rouse us? As the man continued to advance into the middle of the room, I began to have doubts. The Malays are a modest people, none would ever dare to walk in among sleeping women like this. I was thoroughly awake by now and able to make out the figure of our nocturnal visitor. He was, I regret to say, a Westerner—an Australian who had obviously been imbibing far too much liquor. The only advantage of his being of my race was that it made conversation easier. He staggered up to the side of my bed, clad in the briefest of trunks, murmuring hoarsely: 'Stella darling!' I jumped out of the other side of the bed, hastily wrapping myself in a sheet, sari-fashion, thanking my lucky stars that I was at least wearing a nightgown. This had been a concession to my bedroom mate, the lady missionary, because I usually sleep stark naked in the tropics. 'Stella . . . Stella darling!' insisted the intruder, breathing alcoholic fumes into my face. 'I am *not* Stella—get out of here!' I shouted imperiously, making for the door, which I opened wide. The lady missionary, evidently too frightened to speak, was sitting up in her bed with her hands clasped round her knees. 'Get out,' I repeated firmly, adding emphatically: 'You're drunk.' 'I *know* I'm drunk,' the visitor retorted haughtily as he lurched towards the door; then he paused uncertainly. 'Give me a kiss before I go,' he suggested. 'Certainly not—off with you!' I said with the shoo-ing gesture I normally reserve for blue-bottles. To my relief he tottered forwards and went. I locked the door firmly and rattled it to make sure the operation was complete. 'Well, what did you think of that?' I exclaimed, half-choking with indignation. The lady missionary opened her mouth for the first time. 'I do think it was all rather fun,' she commented without a trace of emotion in her voice.

The flight from Singapore to Djakarta was only a two-and-a-half-hour hop over island stepping-stones that stretched all the way across the Java Sea—olive-green islands thickly covered with jungle vegetation, edged by golden sands as lacy as a Breton pancake. Between them a fleet of tiny outrigger boats: *praus*, with white sails poised at midmast like quills, sailed serenely upon the turquoise sea.

DJAKARTA: EX 'PEARL OF THE EAST'

AS we approached a larger island than the rest, half-hidden by mist and dotted with smoky blue pyramids—smoky and smoking, for Java's volcanoes are very much alive—I looked down a little apprehensively, wondering whether I would succeed in the quests I had set myself.

I had flown half-way round the world to wrest three secrets from this lovely, little-known island. I wished to see the 'Invisible People'—a remote jungle tribe in West Java; I wished to probe into ancient court ceremonial at the palace of the Sultan of Jogjakarta, near the south coast, and I wished to meet Javanese mystics and magicians. My friends in Indonesia had already warned me that these would be very difficult tasks to achieve.

Djakarta lies on the northern coast of Java; this is the flattest and least interesting of her coasts and unfortunately it is this side that confronts visitors arriving from the West. All they see from the aeroplane is a lead-coloured line of sand beaten by waves seeping into a land as flat as Holland. The Dutch settlers who came here in 1618 and founded Batavia must have thought it strangely like their homeland. Scattered clumps of coconut palms like abandoned umbrellas are the only proof that this is no northern territory.

The capital of Indonesia sprawled beneath the aircraft—dirty white, almost treeless and criss-crossed by Dutch-built canals. As we circled lower I saw the lean form of a sedate Dutch Reformed church set beside a park surrounded by villas and bungalows. This used to be the Dutch residential area in the old colonial days when Batavia was still known as 'the Pearl of the East'. It is difficult to think of Batavia, and still less of Djakarta, as a pearl —at least not from a scenic or an architectural point of view. This name must have been bestowed upon the capital as a symbol of the wealth amassed there from the products of the Indonesian archipelago: tea, coffee, tin, palm oil, spices. Spanish, Portuguese, Dutch, and English fought each other bitterly to get this lucrative trade, so much so that even a saint like Francis Xavier, who came here to save heathen souls, could not fail to remark how very rapacious we Christians were.

The moment you land at Djakarta the hot, humid atmosphere seizes you and strips away all energy. None has described it with more admirable effect than Lt. Stockdale, who travelled through Java in 1811:

'Most of the people who live here and even many of the rich who might be supposed to have attained the summit of their wishes have something in their countenance expressive of discontent and dejection which seems a certain sign that all is not right within. After a short residence in this debilitating atmosphere a state of languor and love of inactivity soon overcome all the active powers of the mind and, occasioning a total neglect of exercise, ruin the constitution and induce an absolute repugnance to every kind of occupation. The only resource for those who are in this state of listlessness approaching to torpidity is to seek for relief in society and to endeavour to kill the heavy hours in the most frivolous manner. Smoking tobacco, uninteresting and useless conversation, drinking and card-playing form the sum of their amusements—utterly at a loss how to pass the many tedious hours of the day, only solicitous to make choice of such ways of killing time as least interfere with their beloved state of motionless repose.'

For a long time, the town was a white man's graveyard. Dutch writers remarked that the frequency of deaths in old Batavia: 'renders familiar the mention of them and little signs are shown of emotion and surprise on hearing that the companion of yesterday is today no more. When an acquaintance is said to be dead, the common reply is: "Well, he owed me nothing!" or on the contrary: "I must get my money from his executors." '

The suddenness of deaths in this difficult climate was so much taken for granted that when a European married, the attorney who drew up the contract at the same time made out the will of the newly-wed couple.

Many people think of Java as a land of bright sunshine and limpid blue skies, but this is not so. Java lies near the equator and is therefore nearly always cloudy. The year is divided into wet and dry seasons and in Djakarta you sit and drip in a fairly constant humidity of 99 per cent all the year round.

★   ★   ★   ★

My hosts, Hamid and Zeina, a young Indonesian couple of Arab origin, drove me in a blue Chevrolet from the airport to their bungalow. The only cars imported into Java seem to be large expensive American ones. On the other hand, public transport is totally inadequate for the needs of the three million people who live in the capital.

We drove quickly through the town centre, past the President's palace and the Ministries—all built by the Dutch—to the residential area with its avenues of almost identical bungalows specially built (again by the Dutch) for the tropics. Their small front gardens are filled with magnolia trees and all those tropical plants that are so popular and expensive in England at the moment. It is tantalizing to see them growing so easily out of doors and in such profusion.

Every one of these bungalows has a veranda which is used as a sitting-room where family and friends gather in the comparative cool of the evening to lounge and gossip in rattan-fibre armchairs or to listen to the languorous strains of *kronchung* music broadcast by Radio Djakarta. *Kronchung* is a form of romantic jazz said to have been inspired by old Portuguese airs, but they have also become oddly Hawaïanized during their long stay in the islands. The words of these love ditties are cooed into the microphone by charming Indonesian artists with small, tender voices, not unlike their figures. The typical Indonesian figure is slender, with almost imperceptible curves. The women have tiny bosoms, firm as berries, and equally firm, small buttocks round which their ankle-length sarongs are tightly and unequivocally wound.

There is another veranda at the back of the bungalows, overlooking the strip of back-garden where the large daily washing is hung out to dry. Dishes are also laid out to dry in the sun on a table by the side of the outdoor sink. The washing-up is always performed in the open. Off the L-shaped covered passage at the back are the kitchen, the servants' quarters, and the Malay bathroom.

TAKING A BATH—MALAYAN STYLE

THE Javanese bathe religiously twice a day. Poor people—
that is to say, the greater part of the population—plunge
into the nearest river, where they also perform their natural
functions squatting unconcernedly in mid-stream, sometimes by
the side of their wallowing water buffalo. In Djakarta canals are
used for the same purposes. Unfortunately for tourists, the germ-
and prestige-conscious Republican authorities are trying des-
perately hard to break this age-old, picturesque habit. They have
overheard so many foreigners commenting with short, coarse
laughs on 'those *extraordinary* bathing scenes in the canal—and
right in the very middle of the capital too!' that they have
decided to do away with the whole business, including—if necessary—the canal itself. Prior to closing the canal they dissuade
the natives from using it for intimate purposes and foreigners
from filming or photographing them in the process.

But the Javanese never appear to enjoy a bath as we do.
Nobody ever sings in a Malay bathroom. It is not an inspiring
place. There are no comfortable enamelled baths in which to
soak and sing, dream or read as the fancy takes you. You may
only stand in a Malay type bathroom.

Knowing from previous experience exactly what to expect, I
could not help sighing as I tripped along the covered alley at the
back of my hosts' bungalow to endure my first Malay bath after
an absence of three years.

All these bathrooms are built on the same lines with a total
lack of colour as well as of gadgets that make for comfort and
gaiety. I tripped into the dungeon-like gloom after exchanging
my slippers at the entrance for a communal pair of high-heeled
clogs. Inside, a slimy gutter encircled the stone floor; this is supposed to carry the bath-water to a black hole beneath the tiled

reservoir built at the far end of the bathroom. An alarmingly outsize brown beetle projected a sinister head and waved inquiring
antennae as I approached. One tinful of water splashed upon its
broad carapace caused it to draw in its head and legs before it
sank into inky depths which I did not care to probe. This tin—
an empty margarine tin—served as a dipper; you do not immerse
yourself in a Malay bath—you merely anoint yourself with cold
water from the reservoir, which rarely holds more than three or
four gallons. The Javanese presumably soap themselves over first
with their hands—I never saw any face-cloths. Washing the soles
of one's feet is an acrobatic performance and you risk a nasty fall
every time you stand gingerly upon one leg on the slippery floor
to seize your other foot with a soapy hand. There was no mirror
in the bathroom—there never is—no towel rail, no sponge rack,
but a fleet of soap boxes floating in the overflow from the reservoir. My soap slithered round the edge of the reservoir and
ultimately fell inside, dissolving in a milky mist which I feared
would not be appreciated by those who were waiting to have a
bath after me.

A broom is provided to help you sweep the aftermath of soapy
water into the hole, but however energetically you may proceed,
the water refuses to be hurried along. The best thing to do is to
give it up and effect a cautious retreat in the direction of the towel
hanging on the back of the door beside your dressing-gown. If
you are lucky you may find a fairly dry patch of floor near the
door in which to stand while you rub yourself dry. But I defy
anyone to emerge from a Malay bathroom with both feet *and*
clogs dry. I have never been able to achieve this myself and rare
is the path to a bathroom in Java that is not indicated by a perma-
nent trail of wet footprints.

When you emerge from this ordeal you are expected to carry
your towel out with you and to hang it up to dry in the limp company of those belonging to the other members of the household.
It will hardly be any drier in the late afternoon when it is time for
your second bath, since the atmosphere is so heavily saturated
with moisture.

After the exertions of a Malay bath, people loaf on the veranda in their dressing-gowns, sip a cup of tea or coffee, and receive guests. It is obvious from what I have just said about these tropical bathrooms that ladies cannot indulge in glamorous negligées in this part of the world where there is a complete absence of lace and frills. In the middle of the afternoon, the verandas of most Indonesian bungalows and hotels are filled with dishevelled men and un-made-up women. This old-established custom was remarked upon in 1898 by a scandalized American lady visitor with the incredible name of Elizah Ruhamah Scidmore, who noted in her diary:

'Woman's vanity and man's conventional ideas evidently wilt at the line and no formalities pass the equator when distinguished citizens and officials can roam about hotel courts in pajamas and bath slippers, and bare-ankled women clad only in the native sarong or skirt and a white dressing jacket go unconcernedly about their affairs in public places. It is a deshabillé beyond all burlesque pantomime and only shipwreck on a desert island would seem sufficient excuse for women being seen in such an ungraceful, unbecoming attire—an undress that reveals every defect while concealing beauty!'

The above remarks still apply to many European—especially Dutch—women, who are generally more in need of foundation garments than the slim Javanese. But foundation garments in tropical heat must be a terrible form of torture. I do not know whether anybody wears them but no woman looks as if she does. In the kampongs, Javanese peasant women wear brassieres as a form of outward apparel with nothing else over them.

SERVANTS GALORE

I WAS stopped on the way back to my bedroom by the youngest maidservant of the house; she went by the name of Gendo, which means 'young girl', although she was sixteen years old and for ever falling in love with the neighbours' 'boys'. Gendo wanted to know whether I preferred coffee to tea at this time of the afternoon; both were available: a large pot of tea was kept in the kitchen and a large pot of coffee stood on the little rattan-fibre table at the back, for the members of the household or their guests to help themselves. My hosts had two servants and a 'boy'. They were always ready to respond to our summons with cat-footed alacrity. My hosts allowed them two hours off every afternoon and paid for their annual two weeks' holiday—unusually generous treatment for employers. During meals Gendo squatted deferentially in the doorway leading from the dining-room to the kitchen, waiting for orders and listening to our conversation.

Gendo and her mother, the cook, had worked for Hamid's relatives in East Java; Djakarta was new and frightening and they did not like to wander off and explore it on their own. Gendo might have been more venturesome had her mother not been there; she had a coquettish way of swaying her hips and smiling at gentlemen visitors to the house that implied she was ripe for a lover. Are Javanese women passionate? This is a difficult subject to investigate. 'They are too passive,' declared a young male acquaintance of mine from the Middle East; 'They are very intense,' said Zeina, adding that she had known Javanese girls to swoon from suppressed emotion at the feet of the man they loved. (Similar cases, however, have been heard of in Europe, particularly in societies where girls and boys do not mix freely.) Captain Cook found that the Javanese women made 'most excellent, tender nurses'. I can well believe that they could be very tender; they have such soft little hands, such smooth skins, such cuddly little feet and winning ways . . . but passionate? They are so slow-moving, almost reptilian at times. Nevertheless, Gendo's approach to the males who came to our household sometimes made me wonder. Nowadays, however, there are less domestic intrigues than in the old days. An eighteenth-century English writer observed that Javanese women were terribly jealous of their slaves (probably with good reason, as in certain Moorish households I have known).

'Among other methods of torturing them [he wrote], they make the poor slave girls sit before them in such a posture that they can pinch them with their toes in a certain sensible part which is the peculiar object of their vengeance, with such cruel ingenuity that they faint away by excess of pain.'

Besides gay Gendo and her watchful mother, there was Djuri, the fifteen-year-old 'boy'—a recent acquisition. Hamid wanted somebody to clean his car for him every morning and deliver messages, since many people are still not on the telephone. This 'boy' had been recommended by another group of relatives. The Javanese are constantly surrounded, supported, scolded, and supervised by inquisitive hordes of aunts, uncles, and cousins to the umpteenth degree. I suspect these particular relatives had wanted to rid themselves of the 'boy', for he was quite stupid. He came from Central Java and had absorbed the defects, but not the qualities, of the Central Javanese. He was apathetic, easily imposed upon, and incapable of using his common sense, and yet my hosts never chided him. When he exasperated them, as he did so often, they would only look at each other and shake their heads sorrowfully. There was never any question of dismissing him. Unknown to me, until I pressed them on the subject much later, his employers were undertaking a long-term process of reform, gradually coaxing Djuri to use what little grey matter nature had endowed him with.

The day I arrived I gave the 'boy' a letter to take to a friend of

mine only a few streets away to inform him that I would be calling that evening. Three hours later, I found the undelivered letter
hidden under an inkstand in the drawing-room. The 'boy' then
confessed that he had searched for the street in vain. He could not
read and he had not thought of asking anyone for its whereabouts
so he gave up the quest and came back without a word of explanation.

Two days after my arrival, Zeina sent the 'boy' to stand in a
queue for *gado-gado* (this is a dish of bean shoots and other vegetables mixed with peanut sauce. It is typically Javanese but there
is a famous Chinaman in Djakarta who makes it so well that
Indonesian customers line up for it regularly every day). We
waited and waited but the 'boy' never returned; in the end,
Hamid set off in the car to find out what had happened. He ultimately discovered that the 'boy' had let everybody else push in
front of him, he was now the last in the queue and there was no
gado-gado left. We were all disappointed, but the 'boy' was not
rebuked: foreigners treat their servants with far more asperity
and in consequence they are often faced with enormous difficulties. The latest Egyptian Ambassador and his wife were reported to have behaved so arrogantly towards their Javanese
domestic staff, including the gardener, that they handed in their
collective notice.

There are servants galore in Java; if you employ several, none
of them will be overworked and they will all be happy. They
will be for ever in your way, they will often behave in the most
extraordinary manner (by Western standards), and to begin with
they will be hopelessly inefficient, but if you settle down in Java
you will have plenty of time in which to train them, and the
results can be rewarding. Since my return I have heard that
Gendo has learned how to read and write, and Djuri is improving
daily.

SHARING BOWLS OF RICE

THE friends I was staying with belonged more or less to what we would call the upper middle class. Hamid supplemented his meagre salary as a Member of Parliament with his lawyer's practice. Both Hamid and Zeina had been educated at Dutch schools and they often lapsed into the Dutch language between themselves or when they were speaking to friends of their own generation and status. Both of them spoke English very well, although they had only spent three weeks in England—where they had shivered all the time (they came during one of our less enchanting months of June), and they were thankful to return to the heat of Djakarta. They were both of Arabian origin. Zeina's ancestors had originally come from the Hadramaut, but intermarriage with Indonesians had not effaced Arabian features and mannerisms.

Their three adorable children, aged from ten to six, Atika, Mahir, and Adila, would have taught me Indonesian (and learned English themselves) very rapidly had my mind not been full of so many other subjects. My limited vocabulary was only just sufficient to allow me to ask the servants for the few things I wanted and to bargain with the *betjak* boys. But Atika and Adila were determined that I should not leave the shores of Java before I learned *something* Javanese to show my fellow countrymen when I got back. They followed classical Javanese dancing lessons once a week and they eventually decided that I must be taught at least how to move my head slowly from side to side in the regal manner of *Srimpi* dancers. The children left for school at seven-thirty in the morning by *betjak*. (There was no class after lunch.) As soon as they returned, at noon, and saw me reading or writing on the veranda, they would fling down their satchels, run up to me, seize my heavy Western head between their leaf-like golden hands and twist it round—gently but firmly—watching me all the while with an expression of deep concern, until I 'got it right'. Then they would joyfully clap their hands, exclaiming: '*Bagus* (good), Auntie Nina!' and skip off to inform their parents that I was making progress in the delicate Eastern art of making one's head appear to be as flexible as a nodding flower.

Atika and Adila dressed in the traditional Javanese sarong for their dancing lessons. This cotton garment—the best ones are hand-painted—is wrapped under the armpits leaving the neck and shoulders bare except for ornaments, and it extends sheathlike to the feet. The servants wore the modern *kain*, which is wrapped round the waist and worn with a long-sleeved jacket called a *kebayah*. This jacket is a late addition to the national dress and it always looks like an afterthought for it seldom matches the colours of the *kain*.

Zeina had a dressmaker who made her European-style clothes. She only wore her *kain* when she went visiting her more orthodox friends or at official receptions when national dress is rightly expected of the ladies. A little while after my arrival, Hamid and Zeina were invited to a formal dinner party at a political leader's house in honour of some visiting Burmese; after this, we were all going on to a 'modern' friend's house to dance. In between these two occasions, Zeina effected a quick change. She went out to dinner *à la Javanaise*, in *kain* and *kebayah*, but she drove herself back in the car immediately after to put on a short evening dress. How astonished the Burmese would have been to see the transformation!

Hamid and Zeina were strict enough Muslims not to stock or drink alcohol at home, but this was a *very* modern—therefore a cocktail—party. I noticed the presence, upon this and subsequent social occasions, of several Americans whose free and easy informal ways made them fairly popular with the Indonesians. I am sorry to be unable to report the same of my fellow countrymen. They are fewer in number, it is true, and they are not so wealthy, but one cannot help feeling that these drawbacks *could* be partly compensated for by an open, friendly approach. Indonesians flock to our British Council reading rooms and are avid for English books when they can get them. It would pay us in terms of future friendship to send them our literature *free*. Our books are worth more in this connection than the few rather rigid representatives we have out there.

A few days later I was invited to a more old-fashioned gathering. It was an interesting experience but one which I would not care to repeat. The women were segregated from the men during most of the evening, the buffet was temperate and we were obliged to sit through a modern puppet show interspersed with a generous sprinkling of moral 'messages'. Puppet shows have their points—I shall describe the traditional performances later on—but they *are* long and at a party they tend to make one feel restive.

The Javanese adore parties but they never play games as do so many English people on these occasions. I am sure they would find this very childish. *We* find their receptions boring, with nothing to do but sit about and be stuffed with sweet, sticky rice. Javanese *slametans* are given on the occasion of a birth, or a circumcision ceremony, a wedding or a birthday. Few parties are ever given for the sheer fun of it. 'What is the party *for*?' asked the guests invited to an English friend's house in Jogjakarta. In the end, the hostess remembered that the date coincided with her mother-in-law's birthday. This announcement was greeted with relief, for everybody was bursting to know the *real* reason for the invitation.

Mahir, Atika, and Adila went to an unending series of birthday parties while I was in Djakarta and Hamid complained that having to provide so many presents was a drain on his income. Adults have to send baskets of flowers to the hosts of *their* parties —another very expensive item—and of course Mrs. X is always very careful not to send a cheaper-looking gift than Mrs. Y next door.

Snobbery is universal. I can never understand why the English have been accused of it as if it were something peculiar to them.

In Djakarta there are child snobs too; they look down upon those children who drive up to school in vulgar *betjaks* instead of large American cars. In addition they are colour-conscious and mock those who have darker skins than theirs. Light skins are highly thought of; humble peasant women and their little girls dab white powder on their faces in the innocent belief that this helps to make them more attractive.

Dutch snobbery among the *nouveau riche* of Batavia used to go to quite incredible lengths. Social life in the eighteenth century for instance was hedged about with the most absurd regulations resulting from the snobberies of the day. The women were worse than the men. A contemporary writer assures his readers that:

'The ladies most tenaciously insist upon every prerogative attached to the station of their husbands; some of them, if they conceive themselves placed lower than they are entitled to, will sit in sullen and proud silence during the whole evening. It does not infrequently happen that two ladies of equal rank, meeting each other in their carriages, neither will give way though they may be forced to remain for hours in the street. . . .'

Things got to such a pass that the Dutch Government had to regulate the dress of the East India Company's employees and of their wives according to their grade. Velvet coats (one would have thought they would be too hot for this climate anyway) were absolutely forbidden to anyone under the rank of senior merchant. The Act embodying all these regulations runs to no less than one hundred and thirty-nine articles, and one can imagine how its authors must have sweated over them. In the eighth article it is laid down that 'little chaises for children drawn by the hand must be gilt or painted in the exact proportion of the parents' rank'. Article Thirty-one decrees that nobody inferior to a merchant shall use a parasol or umbrella in the neighbourhood of the castle, except when it rains. (Since it rains during six months of the year this was not such a hardship.) Ladies whose husbands

C   33

were below the rank of Counsellor of India could not wear at one time jewels of greater value than six thousand dollars; wives of senior merchants were limited to four thousand and others to three and one thousand dollars' worth. I hope that these instances will not give any ideas to our own Chancellor of the Exchequer! The two following restrictions, however, would not be practical nowadays, for even our few remaining millionaires would never think of making such a public exhibition of their wealth: Article Forty-nine of the Batavia Act permitted ladies of the higher ranks to go abroad with three female attendants who might wear ear-rings of single, middle-sized diamonds, gold hairpins, petticoats of gold silver, or silk cloth, jackets of gold or silver gauze, chains of gold or beads and girdles of gold—*but* neither pearls nor diamonds nor any other kind of jewels in the *hair*! Article Sixty-five severely stipulates that none but the persons of the very highest rank are allowed to have trumpets, clarions, or drums among the music with which it is customary to entertain guests during dinner. The most favoured personage of all was the Director of the region of Suram. *He* was allowed to be preceded by bearers carrying four fans made with the feathers of the Bird of Paradise and cow hair, with golden cases and handles. Not even the Sultan of Jogjakarta would dream of such fabulous luxuries in these austere days!

★　　★　　★　　★

Most of the flowers that Zeina sent to the friends who invited her to their parties were bought from her next-door neighbour, a young Chinese woman and an expert orchid-grower. It was in Mrs. Yen's back-garden that I first saw Java's famous Moonlight Orchid, a temperamental bloom that resents being plucked from its tree-trunk home. The Moonlight Orchid grows in heavy clusters of small brilliantly white flowers that glow with a silvery radiance—hence their name.

One morning, President Sukarno called to see Mrs. Yen's orchids. He has a summer palace (once used by Dutch Governors and by our Sir Stamford Raffles) in the hills of Bogor, in the centre of one of the most famous botanical gardens in the world. Perhaps they have stimulated his interest in flowers, or maybe this has been infused into him by the pink water-lilies that float upon the lake beneath his bedroom window. Water-lilies grace peasants' ponds as well as the President's lake; I have seen them rising with regal stateliness between the humblest bamboo dwellings. These lilies open like a bright message of hope for little more than an hour in the cool early hours of the morning when the peasants unroll themselves from the bamboo mat that is their only bedding, to take their first bath of the day. After this brief glimpse of the sunlight, the lilies fold themselves up again like tightly wound turbans. Yet flowers are rarely seen in Javanese homes except for the banks of luxurious florists' baskets shown off at parties. How I missed the London barrow boys and their banks of many-hued blooms!

In Djakarta I woke up to a dawn chorus of unfamiliar birdsongs, but to my disappointment none of my Javanese friends could tell me anything about them. They did not know their names, let alone their habits. Nature has lavished her richest gifts upon them and yet they remain incurious and aloof. My hosts could not even tell me the names of the commonest of all Javanese birds, one black and one white, that raid the rice-fields and stand on the water buffaloes' backs to peck the ticks off them. But then one had to remember that they were educated in Dutch schools where they were taught more about life in Holland than in Java. Their children, however, belong to the new generation who are educated in Indonesian schools and it was they who informed me that the black bird who hops on to the *kerbao* is called a *djalak*, while the long-legged white one is known as a *blekok*.

The only birds I recognized were the ubiquitous house sparrows who look exactly the same as ours, but after watching them for some time I discovered that they possess definitely Javanese characteristics. They are far more acrobatic than English sparrows and they climbed up and down the venetian blinds, sometimes even upside down. The sparrows, like the people of this island, are born contortionists.

An endless source of enjoyment for European eyes are the fantastic butterflies, most of them as big as bullfinches. There are butterflies of all colours and also, by way of contrast, velvety black ones that fly with a slow, steady beating of wings not unlike the rhythm of seagulls.

I must confess that I was disappointed with tropical fruits and often longed for a European fruit salad. Most Javanese fruits tend to be mealy, oversweet, and not as varied in taste as ours. The two most popular fruits are bananas and *papayas*; there are many kinds of bananas—from small *pisang susus* (milk bananas) to the valued *pisang rajahs* and the elongated Amboina bananas which are not to be consumed by married women, for they are supposed to render marital relations less harmonious physically. The *papaya* is about the same size as a small melon; it has an orange-coloured pulp and is very insipid. There are pink *jambus*—lovely to look at, but again without much flavour—brown *salacs* covered with scales on the outside like a lizard's skin, mangosteen and custard apples and other fruits which one sees less frequently. Strawberries are grown in the hills but they are not as fragrant as our British berries.

★　　　★　　　★　　　★

Everybody knows that rice is the staple food of the Far East but unless you have eaten it three times a day for weeks on end, as I was forced to do during my travels in Java, you cannot realize just how much rice is actually consumed by the people. Boiled rice is the soggy foundation upon which titbits are added: bean shoots, beans and green leaf vegetables, squares of highly spiced, stringy meat, pickled fish, scraggy pieces of under-nourished chicken, roast peanuts and *sambel*—a fiery sauce of macerated chillies. All food is either tasteless or burning hot; it lacks the finesse of Chinese cuisine, and it is not as satisfying as Indian curries. But I found it healthy and it agreed with me. At least there is nothing synthetic about Indonesian food, no chemical preservatives or colouring matter, no vegetables forced upon artificial fertilizers such as we are obliged to eat in the urban centres of certain countries in the West such as Great Britain.

On the whole the Javanese eat less than we do, and I fear that I did not improve the already none too good reputation of Westerners for I must have appeared to be horribly greedy. My hosts picked at their meals like birds. Nobody could have said that of me!

A TRANCE-DANCE IN THE SLUMS

THE morning after my arrival in Djakarta I took my cine-camera and stopped a *betjak* boy who was pedalling slowly past the bungalow. If you want to get to know Djakarta from the inside this is the ideal mode of transport. *Betjaks* worm themselves into the back alleys of the city and through the slummy kampongs that have invaded its fringes. Driving in an outsize American car cannot give you a true picture of this untidy but fascinating capital. *Betjaks* are tricycles pedalled by barefoot boys with muscular legs and an independent turn of mind. Passengers sit on a leather seat in the front, where there is room for one and a half Europeans, two Chinese, or three Javanese ladies plus a few children. An awning protects you from the glare of the sun. When it rains—and it usually pours when it does—the *betjak* driver stops to tie a ragged curtain in front of you. Thus separated from the outside world you feel like an old-fashioned Chinese bride on the way to her wedding. The curtain flaps in the wind and ultimately sags under the weight of the tropical rain which drips on to your toes until you have to be baled out.

The *betjak* I hailed had lively scenes of volcanic activity painted on its back and sides. Volcanoes and rice-fields—the two main features of a Javanese landscape—figure prominently on most *betjaks*. The more modern ones, however, have been inspired by science fiction and portray winged men engaged in combat with aeroplanes; they have also been given such optimistic names as: 'The Rocket', 'Fast', and 'Superman'. Others are more conservative and adorned with brilliant pagodas, birds, and Chinese junks. Most of the *betjak* owners are Chinese to whom the ragged drivers hand over all their takings at the end of the day except for a few miserable rupiahs.

38

These *betjak* boys are among the poorest members of the community, but they do not appear to be a downtrodden lot. On the contrary they are as perky and impertinent as our Cockneys. I had been advised to bargain with them before being taken—sometimes quite literally—for a ride. It is advisable, but nearly always impossible in a new city, to know exactly where you want to go, because no *betjak* boy will ever admit he does not know where such and such a street is located. He embarks upon the journey obviously expecting a sudden revelation on the way; when this is not vouchsafed to him he stops abruptly, removes his coolie hat, and leaves you in the middle of the street while he sits fanning himself on the kerb, looking hurt.

'Well, now,' I said to my *betjak* driver, 'first I want to go to the canal—how much?' The *betjak* boy shrugged his shoulders; 'The usual fare,' he replied. There is never anything 'usual' about *betjak* fares, so I ignored this remark. It was now up to me to make a suggestion. 'Four rupiahs?' The *betjak* boy roared with laughter as if I had made the wittiest remark he had ever heard in his life. Then he suddenly became deadly serious and shook his head. 'Five rupiahs,' he retorted. 'No, four rupiahs,' I insisted. The *betjak* boy gave me a pitying smile and half-turned to go. I turned too, in the opposite direction, and began to walk firmly down the road. A few moments later 'The Rocket' came careering alongside me. '*Boleh*—agreed—four rupiahs,' said the *betjak* boy with an affable smile, beckoning me to climb into his bright red and blue vehicle. From then on we were friends and he showed off his prowess by darting in and out of the traffic with alarming speed, always only just avoiding a headlong collision with large American cars; finally, I shut my eyes every time we reached a main thoroughfare and murmured a prayer suitable to a rapidly approaching journey's end.

After I had filmed the bathing and washing scenes in the canal of which the authorities so heartily disapprove, I asked the *betjak* boy to take me to the fish market at the foot of the old Dutch fortress by the harbour. This is the most picturesque and carefree quarter of Djarkarta. Splendid sailing boats glide along here, *praus* with large eyes painted upon them so they can 'see their way' at night and large boats from far-away Macassar and the Spice Islands, with billowing sails like the galleons of old. The harbour is carefully watched by the police for there is said to be a vast amount of smuggling between this coast and Singapore. Some of the crews admittedly look piratical, while others, especially those from the smaller *praus*, merely look indolent and easygoing. The *prau* is the only home they know; sea-gipsies, they have been called, for they wander from port to port and creek to creek between the islands of the Java Sea as far as Borneo to the north and down to Bali, Lombok, and Flores in the west. Sea-gipsies! What a world of romance in that name and in that life! I should have liked to join them for six months or a year; after that, I should probably be lost to civilization. These islands have a strange enchantment about them and alluring goddesses are said to live in the depths of the ocean.

The harbour was odorous and hot so I soon requested the *betjak* boy to drive me to the quieter back streets. He plunged unconcernedly through stagnant pools beside overcrowded bamboo shacks where naked children waddle in mud and goodness knows how many people live in one room.

When I spied a man frying *saté* on the kerb I stopped the *betjak* at once. My driver joined a group of his cronies who were seated upon a box eating noodles out of a bowl, while I approached the *saté* vendor. *Saté* bought on the streets is the Javanese equivalent of fish and chips; you are not considered to be very high up in the social scale if you are caught in the act of eating it on the pavement.

Of course you can eat *saté* in private houses too but it never tastes quite the same indoors. You miss the street noises and pungent odours which are part and parcel of the genuine *saté* atmosphere. Zeina once kindly bought *saté* for me off a street vendor but she made us eat it respectably in the dining-room; the brief journey from the street to the house raised its social status but decreased its personality. Bourgeois *saté* is good but unexciting.

Saté, quite simply, consists of small pieces of grilled meat pierced on to a bamboo skewer and dipped into hot sauce. I know of two kinds of sauce, but there must be more: one is sweet and tastes like liquorice; the other, my favourite, is peanut sauce. *Saté* resembles the Middle Eastern kebab but the meat—true to Javanese custom—is cut up into elfin portions.

The *saté* vendor does not grill his meat until a firm client appears on the scene. 'How many?' he asked me as I stood looking down at his compact equipment. 'Twelve,' I said. 'That will be five rupiahs,' he stated. As soon as I nodded my agreement he sprung into fascinating action. The *saté* vendor squats during the entire operation (the Javanese find this uncomfortable posture relaxing and they keep it up for hours). He squats between two boxes divided into compartments like miniature cupboards; the long bamboo pole slung across them rests on his shoulders when he decides to carry his goods to another location or walk the streets and cry his wares, which he does in a high-pitched voice, sometimes leaving out the first syllable and shouting: 'é—é!' At other times, he shouts: 'Sa . . .' followed by a squeaky: 'é!' after a long pause.

From the lower compartment of one box, the *saté* vendor scooped out a handful of pieces of charcoal which he dropped one by one like lumps of sugar on top of the faintly glowing embers of a small brazier in front of him. He leaned over and sighed life into them gently, rhythmically, until they began to crackle. Then, from the upper compartment of one of the boxes he brought out a handful of meat-filled skewers upon a little plate. The opposite box was crammed with rows of mysterious bottles (probably bought or bartered from his itinerant colleague who walks the streets crying: '*Bo-tol!*'). These contained condiments which he poured into a saucer, a few drops at a time, and then mixed with a bamboo stick. After another more vigorous blow over the charcoal he began to grill the skewers of meat, turning them deftly in his feminine fingers until they turned a deep golden brown. When they were done, he dipped them into his sauce, gave them another quick turn over the fire and presented the plateful of *saté* to me with a graceful gesture. The most experienced waiters in our most expensive restaurants are clumsy compared to these humble street cooks of Djakarta's slums. While I feasted, the *saté* vendor tidied up his open-air kitchen, put out his fire, raked and swept up the ashes and rearranged his doll's house cupboards. I am sure that if an enterprising Javanese were to start a portable *saté* business in the streets of London he would make a fortune. On the other hand, he would probably die of cold long before this achievement.

While I was delicately biting off the last piece of meat from the last skewer—an operation which must be performed with the skewer held at right angles or you risk piercing the back of your throat, with fatal results—I heard a sudden pulsating of drums from behind a group of bamboo dwellings. A kampong wedding perhaps, or a *slametan* in honour of a new addition to the already overcrowded population? Forgetting all about my *betjak* I rushed off in the direction of the primitive music. Such drums as these are only heard in country kampongs or in the slums where they have been brought by people who until recently were jungle-dwellers. With their drums and their beliefs in spirits and magic they have coaxed the jungle into the city. The scene I was about to witness was a throwback to a sometimes terrifying world which is as foreign to 'progressive' Indonesians like my hosts as it was to me.

A knot of ragged *betjak* boys and a few women with naked babes astride their hips had gathered round two oddly assorted individuals. 'There's going to be a *kuda lopeng*—a "dance of the human horse",' one of the bystanders informed me. 'It's been ordered for a birthday *slametan*,' added another. I was the only stranger in the crowd but nobody stared or objected to my presence. They were too engrossed by the extraordinary performance to which we were all being drawn as by a magnet.

The elder of the two men was thin and bent, with matted hair falling over bony shoulders; his face was haggard and his dark eyes sunken, but they shone with an unnatural brilliance—like

42

those of North African snake-charmers. A few feet away from him a young man crouched shivering as in an epileptic fit. He was sitting astride a hobby horse—a flat frame made of bamboo and painted in black, with a gaudy fringe tied on to the mane. Somebody tossed a bundle of hay into a corner; it was one of the essential props. Three musicians sat with their backs against a bamboo house beating drums of different sizes with long, nervous fingers. One of the drums was long and narrow like those one sees in India and in Arab countries. Only 'primitive' people can play drums as these men did. They are closer to vibrations which the town-bred can no longer capture and which would no longer inspire him; they have inner aerials that enable the rhythm of the drums to rouse a tangle of wild emotions and memories of the long-lost childhood of the human race. Their playing made one tingle with pleasure but also with fear for it conjured up unseen forces; none could be sure whether they were good or evil forces, but all watched tensely with a half-conscious, undefinable feeling of guilt.

The old man was holding a whip. He stiffened and drew himself up, fixing the boy with his glittering, hypnotic eyes. The drums softened instantly and melted into the background where they continued to echo as faintly as a human heart during the entire exhibition. The boy raised his eyes towards the sorcerer and an anguished silence ensued. Nobody in the audience stirred. Whether we wanted to or not we had all been drawn into the magic circle. We were the involuntary prisoners of that fearsome creature with matted hair and talon-like hands. We were assisting him with an unrealized force latent in every one of those present. Throb throb, throb throb went the drums like metronomes wrapped in velvet. Then the old sorcerer let out a bestial snarl accompanied by a crack of his whip; we started and fell back a pace or two. The instant he heard the snarl the young man responded with a half-choked sound like a horse's neigh. The sorcerer cracked his whip again and shouted an order in a high quavering voice. The boy-horse approached the bundle of hay. Again he neighed—now there was no mistaking the sound—and then—I could hardly believe my eyes—he bent forward and began to munch the hay.

After two or three minutes, the sorcerer shrieked another command; the boy-horse reacted instantly and began to rear and prance like a circus pony. At another crack of the whip he galloped round the sorcerer raising clouds of dust and shaking his long black hair out of his eyes. The sweat trickled off his body in slow globules. His breathing—which was more like snorting—became heavier. All his muscles appeared to have lengthened; even his face had narrowed and looked curiously equine.

The performance must have lasted for about fifteen minutes, perhaps less, but it seemed timeless like eternity. It ended as abruptly as it had begun. The boy-horse suddenly uttered a pitiful cry and rolled over on the ground panting, his body moist with perspiration, his eyes staring at the sky with the fixity of the demented. The sorcerer watched him for a few moments with the triumphant intensity of a beast that has vanquished its prey. Then he stepped forward and bent over the writhing form, whispering a magic formula from his armoury of secret incantations. Only now was I aware of the fact that the drums had stopped their insistent beating. The whispering of the sorcerer was like a hissing of serpents. Little by little the twitching body of the boy-horse began to quieten down. The muscles relaxed, the convulsed face became smooth and rounded as before, the breathing subsided—almost ceased.

Before the crowd dispersed, one of the drummers rose and walked round to collect a few rupiahs; the sorcerer appeared to be oblivious of our presence—he continued to bend over the boy, who now appeared to be sleeping peacefully. Somebody nudged my arm. It was my *betjak* driver. He was smiling and his black teeth shone like the pips in a water-melon. 'What do you think of the *kuda-lopeng*?' he asked me. 'It was good,' I replied, not knowing enough Indonesian to express myself more subtly. The *betjak* boy shrugged his shoulders with the casualness of a connoisseur. 'I have seen better,' he told me. 'Still, it wasn't bad. It was genuine anyway. Sometimes the boy just pretends he's in a trance. They can't always go into a real one and that makes it awkward for everybody, since they earn their living that way. Oh, but of course the old *dukun* has a few sidelines. He makes and sells medicines and amulets too—he's no fool!'

I arrived back at the bungalow late for lunch. Hamid and Zeina were a little concerned—they were afraid that I had got irretrievably lost in the tortuous kampong alleys. They were amazed when I told them that I had been watching a *kuda-lopeng*. They had never seen such a performance, nor known of its existence in the capital.

We were invited to a preview of a new Indonesian film that afternoon. It had been directed by a friend of my hosts, Ismail, one of the best directors in Indonesia, who had recently returned from a year's training in Hollywood. Oddly enough this film dealt with the folly of superstitious folk who go to consult a *dukun*, a sincere man but a quack who meddles in everybody's affairs and almost ruins their lives. Since the film had to have a happy ending, the *dukun's* customers came to their senses and the *dukun* ended by confessing that he was a well-meaning deceiver. Among his clients were educated people, even a Member of Parliament. In the course of my subsequent travels through Java, I met a variety of magicians and fortune-tellers. The fact that some of them possess unusual powers—like the sorcerer I had seen that very morning—is beyond any doubt, but in no field is the possibility of delusion so vast. That is what Ismail was trying to bring home in his film with its 'social message' for the masses. In spite of it, however, I am convinced that *dukuns* will continue to be popular in Indonesia for a very long time to come. It will take more than one film to break people from traditional habits and to prompt them to think for themselves.

THE MYSTERY OF THE MAGIC DOLL

ARAFA, the young Indonesian who had taken me to a *pen-chak*, or Javanese display of the art of self-defence, suddenly bent forward and whispered: 'Would you like to see a Ni Tuwong séance? I can show you one in a kampong this afternoon.' 'Ni Tuwong? Do you mean the Magic Doll? I thought that was a thing of the past—of course I should love to watch it,' I excitedly replied. I never would have thought that this curious custom had survived the revolution and the wave of modernism that followed it. Many more similar surprises were in store for me.

After lunch, Arafa and I made off for an obscure kampong at the edge of a country town about fourteen miles west of Djakarta. It was a Thursday—or, as it is called in the Javanese calendar, Friday eve, and the Ni Tuwong ceremony, as usual, was to be conducted in a cemetery. We sauntered through the sun-baked streets to a shady hinterland of coconut palms where the peasants live. Perhaps the stillness of their nature is a reflection of the timid shadow in which they spend so much of their existence. The crude verandas of the houses on piles were filled with sleeping forms curled up in sarongs. Ducks were dozing under the piles and the rosy-breasted pigeons in cages hoisted high above the rooftops were lulled to silence in the airless atmosphere.

The cemetery lay at the back of the kampong, nearly a mile from the town. It was set upon a mound like a prehistoric tumulus, in the middle of gleaming rice-fields. Coconut palms formed a dense canopy over this peaceful oasis and an outer rim of cambogia trees spread fragrant cream blossoms above the plain Muslim tombstones. These cambogia trees are always associated with cemeteries in the country; they have no leaves and the twisted branches are the most lifeless-looking objects in Java, where no tree ever sheds its foliage. They would look sadly skeletal if those waxen flowers were not there to remind us that life can spring from death. The striking contrast between the apparently dead branches and the blooming flowers is in itself a message of hope in resurrection—a silent message suited to the quiet, undemonstrative Javanese, who value unspoken meditation more than the crude finality of words.

A few kampong women and girls were wending their way to the cemetery over the ridges that separate rice-fields like the leading in stained-glass windows. We removed our shoes, for our feet sank up to our ankles in the soft mud, and took our place in the leisurely procession.

At the summit of the cemetery, under the tallest, straightest palms, a knot of old women bent over a tombstone were talking gravely in low tones. They were arranging some object at their feet with the fussy, impatient gestures common to old ladies the world over. A group of younger women, their eyes glistening with excitement, were seated cross-legged on the ground, waiting for the elders to complete whatever they were doing. Faint wisps of incense rose from little brass bowls placed round the tombstone, which had been filled with the rose petals and pandan leaves used for offerings to gods and to the spirits of ancestors.

The old women, their task completed, huddled beside the object of their attentions. Two of them bowed their white heads and began to intone a mournful incantation. In the centre, propped up against a tombstone and now clearly visible to us all, was the doll figure which was to be animated by the spirit called Ni Tuwong. The doll looked as grotesque as a Guy Fawkes effigy, with its coconut-shell head upon which great white eyes had been outlined in chalk; bamboo brooms served for arms and the bamboo frame that passed for a body was wrapped in a sarong that had been specially 'stolen' for the occasion. I do not know why this should be so, but Ni Tuwong must always wear a stolen garment.

The incense-burning and incantations had started a couple of hours before we arrived. Now the shrivelled old women who were conducting the ceremony decided that the doll had remained in the cemetery long enough for the spirit of Ni Tuwong to have entered into it and they made a sign to Arafa, whom they evidently knew well, to step forward and carry it down to the kampong for them. He took the ludicrous bundle in his arms and strode ahead of us with a wild glint in his eye, oblivious to everything and everybody around him. One of the old women jumped up with the sprightliness of a tree squirrel and stepped behind Arafa; she held a mirror clasped close to her breast. The other cronies followed chanting and the girls brought up the rear, bringing the bowls of incense with them. The atmosphere had become charged with electricity as before a violent thunderstorm. All the way from the cemetery to the edge of the kampong, where Arafa stopped and laid down the doll, I had the uncomfortable feeling that there was an unseen presence among us.

Other kampong people came out of their houses and gathered round us as we squatted in front of the image. Arafa set it up against the trunk of a coconut palm and the girls rearranged the bowls of incense round the tree. All chatting ceased as one of the old women held the mirror in front of the stolid coconut head which stared uncomprehendingly at its reflection. Set down in writing, cold, after the event, this scene may sound absurd, but it was not; it was uncanny. Could the shadow of a passing butterfly have been responsible for the change of expression that had come over the doll's coconut face? For there was no doubt that it had altered. It was not a dead and inert object any longer. The lumpy, fibrous head began—almost imperceptibly at first— to loll first to one side, then to the other. The old woman with the mirror muttered to the doll in affectionate, urging tones— was I mad or was this a collective hallucination? The doll head moved quite distinctly; it turned slowly away from the mirror and stared at the eager young girls assembled before it. The broomstick arms began to twitch convulsively—yet there was nobody behind the tree, no obvious agent whom one could point to as the cause of this plainly visible movement.

The old woman lowered the mirror and murmured to the girls behind her. They nudged one another and began to whisper.

At last one of them, a little bolder than the rest, raised her voice and addressed a question to the doll. Her companions covered their mouths to stifle their nervous giggles. Very slowly Ni Tuwong turned her head from one side to the other in a negative gesture. 'She says no—you will not be married this year,' interpreted the crone. Another girl now spoke to Ni Tuwong. All eyes were fastened upon the crude image as it jerked its head up and down. 'Good, her mother will recover from her illness,' commented a girl at my side.

The questions now came tumbling one after the other and the doll rolled its head and moved its arms quicker and quicker as if inspired. Suddenly, Arafa bent over and put a question to it. 'Ni Tuwong,' he said—loudly enough for all to hear—'Ni Tuwong, what new friend have we here today?' There was a silence as the doll cocked its ludicrous head to one side. Then, to my horror and amazement it bent forward and pointed one of its long, skinny broomstick arms straight at *me*! Everybody turned to look. Mesmerized, I stared back at the blank coconut face twenty feet away from me and felt the blood being drained from my cheeks. Ni Tuwong had leant forward so abruptly that she had toppled over. She remained quite still, face downwards, with arms outstretched. 'She has left us—it's all over,' sighed one of the girls. There was a stir in the crowd as people began to rise and move away. Glasses of tea were passed round to those who had stayed behind. Nobody was interested in the lifeless image which was left to lie at the foot of the tree like a forgotten plaything.

Arafa came over to sit beside me. He was laughing. 'Don't you think that final act was cute?' he said in his American English. I could not bring myself to laugh with him. In spite of the heat, I was shivering violently. 'We must be going—it's getting late,' I said. 'By the way,' cautioned Arafa, 'there's no need to tell anybody in Djakarta about Ni Tuwong. They don't believe in her, you know.'

PART II

IN SEARCH OF THE 'INVISIBLE PEOPLE'

IN SEARCH OF THE 'INVISIBLE PEOPLE'

AFTER I had made inquiries from various sources, I was advised that before setting out for the 'Invisible People's' forest territory in South Bantam, west of Djakarta, it would be as well to discuss the project with the nominal head of this tribe (officially known as Baduis) who live in Djakarta. This was an astonishing piece of news; I would never have thought it possible that such isolated people were in any way connected with the sophisticated capital. But when I was told the name of the 'civilized' Badui family resident in Djakarta, the Djajadiningrats, I was even more taken aback, for the Djajadiningrats are one of the leading families of Djakarta; Hilman Djajadiningrat was the Regent of Bantam at one stage in his career, while his elder brother, Husein Djajadiningrat, is a distinguished Javanese scholar. How were these highly educated people related to the island's most primitive jungle folk? And could it be true, as I had been told, that they are in regular communication with their illiterate brethren?

On the other hand, how was I to approach the Djajadiningrats, who were said to be proud and aristocratic in manner and feudal in their ways, in order to discover the truth? A direct, Western type of approach was completely out of the question.

Fortunately for me, one of the younger members of the family, Kayse Djajadiningrat, a civil servant, belonged to the same political party as that of my host—the P.S.I. or Indonesian Socialist Party—and they knew each other well. It was therefore suggested that I should seek Kayse's advice in the first place. I paid him a formal visit at his office in the Ministry of Communications. Thanks to my introduction from his friend, he received me with an affable smile. As soon as I set eyes on him, I realized that Kayse was different from all the other Javanese I had met. . . . His eyes were unusually brilliant, and more prominent than those of the average Javanese. The pupils were rounder, the whites whiter, and the arc of the eyebrows was more pronounced. At the same time they were curiously familiar. As we talked I searched frantically in my memory, turning out drawer after drawer of recollections to find the analogy I wanted. In the end I found two—one feminine and one masculine. The feminine one was the venerated Romanesque image of Santa Maria de Ujué in Spanish Navarre. She too has these glistening black, carefully outlined eyes. The masculine analogy was a picture of a Tibetan seer, meditating in a forest clearing, his eyes fixed in front of him, wide-open and all-seeing, which I had come across in a textbook on Oriental art. Later on, in the depths of the Badui forests, my mind was to swing back to Tibet time and time again—but that is another story.

Kayse Djajadiningrat's face was firmly chiselled; he had a particularly small mouth for a man, and an abundant shock of straight black hair. I saw him in imagination proudly dressed in the colourful uniform of an ancient sultan's personal guard, with a jewelled *kris*—the Javanese ceremonial dagger—at his embroidered belt. In fact, however, he confronted me in a plain white shirt and in every outward respect behaved like a modern, post-revolutionary Javanese; but when I began to question him cautiously about his family's relationship with the jungle Baduis, this image of an ancient sultan found its rightful place. My intuition had not been at fault, for Kayse is the descendant of a sultan's son-in-law.

In the middle of the seventeenth-century, a Badui boy, the son of a highly respected leader, tiring of jungle life and of the severe laws imposed upon all the members of the tribe, had the temerity to run away and escape to civilization. The details of his flight are unrecorded but eventually he came to the palace of the Sultan of Bantam, who befriended the lad and gave him a job as a stable boy in the royal *kraton* (palace). The Badui had been bold to forsake his people; soon he became even bolder. From stable boy he was promoted to the Sultan's personal retinue, and became the ruler's trusted counsellor, for he was endowed with great natural wisdom. Finally, he was admitted to the inner circle of the court and allowed to marry one of the Sultan's daughters. The aristocratic Djajadiningrats of Djakarta are the descendants of this ambitious and highly successful renegade Badui.

How did the jungle Baduis react to the flight of their leader's son, I asked Kayse. Did he ever try to communicate with them, or was he struck off the tribal records in angry retaliation? Kayse blew a ring of smoke into the air and became absorbed in its slow ascent. There was a faintly sardonic flicker of a smile upon his face as he quietly replied: 'Were the Baduis angry? I do not think so. Anger is considered to be a great sin and they know how to keep their emotions under control. They are said to be primitive, yet they have developed a very strict moral code. They must have been grieved, of course, that a leader's son should find their laws an intolerable burden. But his running away did not, could not alter the fact that he was a leader's son. According to Badui law, the tribal record-keepers were obliged to keep track of him and of his progeny, whatever happens. Their genealogies must be preserved. This, to them, is a sacred task. In consequence they are obliged to keep in touch with us. They have done so ever since.'

'Merely for the sake of the records,' I interjected, amused at the thought of such bureaucracy in the jungle. Kayse paused again before he replied. 'I should have held my tongue,' I thought, 'for it is becoming more and more obvious to me that the Djajadiningrats, far from being embarrassed by their connection with the Baduis, take a serious view of it. I must be careful. This is unfamiliar ground. I am completely out of my depths. If I give the impression of being flippant, I shall not be considered worthy of help.' And, as I had already been warned, an expedition to Badui territory without the prior blessing of a Djajadiningrat would be perfectly futile. It would be difficult to achieve even *with* their blessing.

'The Baduis believe that records are living things,' Kayse began to explain. 'They have significance, both in this life and in the next. My uncle, Professor Husein, will be able to tell you more

55

about these things. I would suggest that you go and consult him. He will advise you about the route. It will be arduous. Nobody outside the tribe has ever seen the Baduis of the inner circle. . . .'

A few days later (it takes time to arrange appointments in Java) I was ushered into Professor Husein's study and introduced to a grey-haired, scholarly-looking gentleman who looked even further removed from the Baduis than Kayse. The Professor was frankly doubtful as to the outcome of my expedition. No woman had ever undertaken it before, and the few men—a Dutch anthropologist and a doctor—who had done so years ago, had never succeeded in locating the 'Invisible People' of the interior. 'They met and conversed with the Baduis of the outer territory, but never the esoteric circle for whom all communication with the outside world is strictly taboo.' For, as he explained, the Baduis are divided into two interdependent clans: an inner clan of forty families, who dress in white, follow rigorous rules of conduct, and never leave their jungle fastness, and an outer clan, who live on the fringes of Badui territory, dress in blue, live less strictly, do a little bartering on behalf of the Invisible Ones, and often act as their external relations officers. In a way, the 'blue ones' are the vassals of the white, who are considered sacred and superior. There is no intermarriage between the two.

'And how does one get to their territory?' I asked the professor a little impatiently. He shook his head gravely. 'Have you got a jeep? Even so, you will only be able to go so far and no more. After that you will have to walk through the jungle. I hear, too, that the wet season has started early this year. It has begun to rain in the hills; it will be very damp and uncomfortable. And you will almost certainly be stopped at the boundary of the Baduis' territory and not permitted to proceed any farther. They are inexorable on that point.'

'What would happen if I insisted? Would they shoot me, or throw poisoned darts at me?'

Professor Husein smiled broadly. 'Good gracious, no. The Baduis would never do anything like that. They are pacifists. They have no weapons whatsoever.'

My admiration for these people was increasing. The more I learned about them, the more I doubted the accuracy of referring to them as 'primitives'.

'But,' I persisted, 'if they would not harm me, then what is there to prevent me from forcing my way through into their territory?'

Professor Husein lowered his eyes and the smile vanished from his face. 'Accidents—mysterious accidents—have occurred to more than one Dutchman who made a similar attempt. But may I ask you this: what would be the use of pushing through? You would find nobody. The Baduis would melt into their jungle. Do not forget that they are called the "Invisible People". They would become indistinguishable from the leaves and creepers of their homeland. They know their jungle. *You* do not. You would be at a hopeless disadvantage.'

I nodded, for I knew enough about jungles to realize the truth of Professor Husein's statement.

'I still want to *try* and see them,' I said.

'You are a determined woman,' remarked the Professor. 'How did you come to hear about the Baduis in the first place?' 'I read about them in Sir Stamford Raffles's *History of Java*. He didn't see them when he was here, but he was very interested He was interested in every aspect of Java, as you know. I was afraid that the Baduis might have become extinct or absorbed into urban life, but a Dutch ethnographer to whom I wrote from England assured me that they were still living in their forests. He didn't hold out any hope of my being luckier than those who have tried before me. And yet, here I am, after having travelled half-way across the world—in part at least for this evidently unattainable objective!'

The Professor studied me closely as I spoke. Then he rose, crossed slowly over to the open window and looked out at the magnolia trees in his garden. 'How curious it is,' he exclaimed after a reflective pause, 'that it has taken nearly one hundred and fifty years—since Raffles wrote his *History of Java*—for the imagination of an English person—and an Englishwoman at that—

57

to be fired by this lonely, ancestral tribe of mine—the Baduis!'
He shook his head wonderingly. 'I suppose Kayse told you that
we have not lost contact with these people? They still come to us
to pay homage—and to protect us in times of danger.' He turned
on his heels and surveyed the bulging bookshelves with a whimsi-
cal smile. 'There are things in our forests,' he commented, 'that
have never yet been written about in books. Perhaps they should
never be put down in writing. Superstitious nonsense, many wise
people would say. But are they so wise as they think? I don't
know. I have been educated in the West, by Westerners. They
have developed—maybe over-developed—my critical faculty!'
He gave a short, hard laugh and shrugged his shoulders.

'Tell me then how I can read the Book of the Forest,' I urged.
The Professor looked pensive. 'I fear they will not open it for
you. The Baduis are secretive even with the Javanese. You,
being a Westerner, are doubly suspect. They are afraid of being
contaminated by anything new. Their life is resolutely turned
towards an archaic past. I have seen places in Europe—houses,
palaces, in which some famous person died and where every single
object is kept exactly as it was at the moment of his death. The
Baduis regard the whole of existence in that light. The rules of
life were laid down once and for all by a remote ancestral divinity
who will one day return to them. In the meantime, nothing must
be disturbed. No new element must be added to what he pre-
scribed for mankind.' The Professor paused and toyed with a
paper-knife on his desk. 'If you have really made up your mind
to go on this wild-goose chase—as I can sense you have,' he said
abruptly, 'then go and see my brother Hilman. He can give you
all kinds of practical information which I do not possess.' He
picked up his telephone and held a brief conversation in Dutch
with his brother. At the end of it, I was given an address, the
Professor hailed a *betjak* outside the gate and off I went for an
interview with a third Djajadiningrat. Would I really be assisted
in my quest, or was I being passed from one to the other because
nobody had the courage to say 'No' to my face? I consoled
myself with the thought that the Djajadiningrats are known to be

strict about their family relationships—that Kayse, being the youngest, could not have done anything of a positive nature before I had been seen and approved by 'the elders', and furthermore nothing could be decided until *both* 'elders' had seen me and agreed on their verdict.

The *betjak* boy pedalled me to an attractive bungalow at the corner of a quiet street in the residential area, not far from the Dutch Reformed church that I had spied from the aeroplane. A soft-voiced servant ushered me into a pleasant, well-furnished sitting-room. There were oil paintings on the walls, Balinese carvings on the polished tables—family photographs in silver frames. Here again, nothing could have been farther away from the jungle, excepting Mr. Hilman Djajadiningrat himself. He bustled into the room a few seconds after I had seated myself on a divan, excusing himself for his scanty knowledge of English; however he seemed to understand all I said without too much difficulty. Hilman was quite different from the other members of the family. He had larger bones, a fairer skin, and an almost Western *bonhomie*, but this could be explained by the fact that he was now a business man and used to meeting many people, especially Europeans, on easy terms.

Like Kayse and Professor Husein before him, Hilman gave me little hope, but he was the first to make a constructive suggestion. 'It's absolutely no good your going alone,' he declared emphatically. 'You just wouldn't see anybody—and nobody has an entry to the Baduis except a Badui. Now, Kayse's mother has a run-away Badui called Japar working on her rubber plantation, about a couple of hours away from Djakarta. He too, like our seventeenth-century ancestor, is the son of a *pu'un* or leader from the inner tribe. He is now an old man and he has adopted the Muslim faith, like us, but he pays occasional visits to his jungle kinsmen and acts as our go-between. He is the obvious person to escort you and to contact the Baduis with a message from me, asking the inner people either to receive you or to go down to the frontier to meet you there if, as I am sure, they do not wish you —as a stranger—to penetrate into their territory. I don't say that it will work—I cannot give orders to the Baduis. I may only ask them for a personal favour.'

Once again, I was baffled by the extraordinary relationship between these two opposite poles of a human race, united in one family. I asked Hilman to tell me more about it. Did he still see the Baduis? Had he ever been into their territory?

Apparently he was too urbanized to be interested in uncomfortable treks through the jungle. When I asked him if he would like to join me and Japar, he threw up his hands in horror. 'I am past all that sort of thing, and besides I have liver trouble,' he protested, although he looked stronger and healthier than I did. The Baduis come down from their hills every year to see him. Since their archaic laws do not permit them to use any other form of transport but their own legs, it takes them some time to cover the odd hundred miles between the jungle and the capital. The moist heat makes the miles seem even longer; the Baduis have to make careful preparations too about their food, for they are most particular and refuse to touch anything except their simple forest diet, apart from salt and smoked fish which is a great as well as a permissible luxury.

'What do they come to see you about?' I asked Hilman.

'According to their laws, the inner people are bound to keep in touch with the leading Badui families, even if they are only nominal, like us. In a way, too, they watch over us.'

'From a distance? Are they clairvoyant?' I queried.

'They appear to be, judging from one or two personal experiences I have had. You have been told, haven't you, how they keep genealogies—family trees, of their leaders? These are living trees—in the sacred place of the Baduis, the *Artjas Domas*, a clearing in a wood at the source of the river Chilibon. Trees have been planted to represent the tribal leaders. Every year the priests of the three villages belonging to the inner circle accompany the leaders to the *Artjas Domas*. There they build themselves a temporary bamboo dwelling in which they remain for three days, fasting and meditating. During this time they remove all moss from the stones which surround the trees and make a careful mental note of the state of their branches. If any of these are withered, this is a sure sign that some misfortune is about to befall a member of the family it represents. Sometimes, lights are seen flickering among the branches—they signify good tidings. It is after their annual visit to the *Artjas Domas* that the inner people make the long journey down to see me, and to convey the "message of the trees". They foretold my appointment as Regent of Bantam and during the revolution they came down to guard me and my household. They posted themselves unobtrusively in the garden and assured me that while they were there, no bullets could pass, for they have the power of diverting missiles containing iron—but,' broke off Hilman, 'you will probably think that all this is gross superstition? All I can say is that one day we *were* shot at, in broad daylight, by Dutch soldiers, but none of us were harmed and furthermore, although we searched afterwards, we never found any trace of the bullets.'

'The bullet-proof theory is not confined to the Baduis,' I remarked; 'it was put into practice by members of Atjehnese secret societies during their struggle against the Dutch at the end of the last century. They were not always successful. But perhaps the Baduis have greater powers. Perhaps, in the words of Frazer, they have "sensitives" among them who "tremble at a touch of nature, and at whose touch nature trembles".'

The conversation ended with Hilman promising to call Japar for an interview in the presence of the Ministry of Information interpreter who would be accompanying me into the interior to explain the purpose of my journey to the various village heads on our way and to discuss the questions of accommodation and bearers for our luggage (the heaviest part of this would be my tape recorder, cine-camera, and tripod). I was quite willing to share the simple food of the villagers in the jungle. Besides, I thought it would make relations smoother if I did not play the part of the superior foreigner who does not deign to share the common people's rice. Later on I was to feel twinges of regret at my decision; a few tins of something tasty would have made jungle meals less functional.

*   *   *   *

A couple of days later, Hilman telephoned to say that Japar had arrived from the rubber plantation. Would I come up to have a talk with him? I called the Ministry interpreter and we went together to Hilman to meet the latest Badui who had chosen the freer life of civilization to the severe containment of the jungle and its (to us) irrational taboos. Many of my European friends think of jungle life as being wild and dissolute. The boot is really on the other foot; as far as Indonesia is concerned, jungle existence is as disciplined as that of an approved home.

After we had sipped iced refreshments in Hilman's lounge, he summoned Japar. The man who now appeared before us, crouching in the deferential *dodok* posture of Javanese inferiors, was in appearance generations closer to the forest aboriginals than his modern master. He was a toothless old man with high cheekbones and slanting eyes that darted at us with reserve and suspicion; he looked as cunning as a European peasant, and although he spoke to Hilman from his servile squatting position on the floor, I noticed that he was not afraid to speak up to him clearly and firmly. He was a subordinate, with the unquestioning respect for authority of a primitive, but when there were tribal points on which he was asked to give his opinion, he was treated as a counsellor rather than a servant, and he replied with dignity.

In the beginning, however, Japar tried by every argument he could think of to dissuade me from undertaking the hazardous expedition to his birthplace. Since he was the only person present who had actually travelled to and from Badui territory, he was supposed to know what he was talking about, and was therefore listened to with attention and respect.

First I wanted to know precisely how near to Badui territory we could get by jeep, and where the route lay. Japar was fairly definite on this. We should drive west as far as Sanggaran, he said, and from there south of Rangkasbitung to a place called Leuwidamar, which was journey's end as far as any vehicle was concerned. From there onwards a jungle track led up the hills to Badui country. It would probably take us a couple of days to reach the border. But it was a very difficult climb, said Japar, with a dubious look in my direction, and he was growing old. He really did not feel he could manage it unless he was carried. 'Surely we will be able to find a couple of bearers at Leuwidamar to carry Japar,' I said.

Japar agreed that this would be possible but, he added in his low, patient voice, there were other drawbacks. Snakes, for instance. There were many large and poisonous snakes in the jungle. I had no reason to doubt the veracity of this statement. Java is famous for its variety of reptiles. On the whole, however, I am fairly indifferent towards snakes. Japar stared at me hopefully, waiting for my reaction to his remark. 'I do not object to snakes; moreover, I am pretty sure that they will be more frightened of us than we of them and so will be careful not to cross our path,' I said. Japar looked crestfallen when this was translated to him. He gazed reflectively at the floor before making his last attempt to prevent me from trying to make contact with his people. 'There are millions of mosquitoes,' he said laconically. 'Well, then, we shall have to take a mosquito net with us,' I retorted. Japar's sallow face broke into a pale, vanquished smile.

We began to discuss the date of our departure. Japar murmured that he would have to obtain his mistress's permission to leave his work on the plantation—Hilman told him that he would settle this himself. Next, I had to find out when the Ministry of Information could put one of their few cars at my disposal. Japar added as an afterthought that it would be a good thing to take some presents with us. We asked him for suggestions, since he knew more about their way of living than we did. He whispered to Hilman, who smiled when he translated Japar's unexpected answer. 'It seems that there are two things which they are very, very fond of and cannot get in the jungle: salt and salted fish. They never accept money—for this is taboo and they never use it. Japar also says that one of the young Baduis has a skin disease, and he thinks it might be a good idea to take him some penicillin.' I was surprised that this innovation should not be on the forbidden list but, as it turned out later, this was Japar's personal suggestion and it proved unacceptable. 'How much salt and fish should we take?' Japar did some quick mental arithmetic. 'There are forty Badui families living in the interior,' he said, 'and I think they would be satisfied if we presented each family with one kilo of salt and a kilo of fish—so that forty kilos of each should be enough.'

It took a further four or five days to settle the last few practical details. For one thing, the Ministry of Information had to write explanatory letters to various authorities on our route, in advance of our arrival, for courtesy—to say nothing of red tape and bureaucracy—demanded that we should pay our respects to the Regent, *Bupati*, *wedana*, and *lurah*, that is the respective heads of the province of Bantam and its sub-divisions.

At last, however, the great day dawned, and the Ministry car came to fetch me—only a couple of hours later than had been stipulated. Apparently it had had to be repaired in haste at the last minute. I felt—and my fears were well founded—that this was not a good augury for its future performance on the bad roads to and from Leuwidamar.

Since so many people like to know what kind of clothes I wear for jungle expeditions, I had better confess right away—even though this may be disappointing—that I left for the wilds in a simple printed cotton, button-through frock that I had bought for one guinea in a popular Oxford Street store. This garment had several advantages: it was printed in dark colours and would not look dirty so soon as a light-coloured dress (only Europeans wear white in the tropics); it was easy to undo for bathing *and* undressing purposes, since there is never much privacy in Java; and lastly it buttoned up fairly high and although I ultimately discovered that Badui women of the outer community are not particular about concealing their charms, we were passing through Muslim areas where I felt that modesty would be *de rigueur*. White women do not enjoy such a high reputation in Java for any individual to risk decreasing it by one iota.

I wore nothing on my head, since we would be walking through shady tropical forests most of the time, according to what Japar had told us. Footwear was more of a problem. I decided to take two pairs of shoes—a pair of lightweight flatties, and a pair of rubber-soled, flat calfskin shoes in case it rained. I was a little dubious about the rubber soles, as well I might.

I packed a minimum amount of objects into a small bag: a change of nylon underwear, a toilet bag, a tin of Elastoplast, and a French skin ointment called 'Mysca' which nobody has ever heard of (in France it is considered old-fashioned), but I have never found anything better for minor trek troubles, from open blisters to insect bites, both of which I am particularly allergic to. Paludrin tablets (thinking of the 'millions of mosquitoes' anticipated by Japar), a tin of digestive powder, in case I was forced to eat too many fiery spices, and a woollen bedjacket in case it was chilly in the hills during the night. I also took a woollen coat, which I used as a blanket. That was the sum total of my luggage, not forgetting my powder compact and lipstick, a necklace and earrings, without which any woman feels lost, even in the jungle.

*   *   *   *

We decided to buy our presents of salted fish at the last possible moment, as we were afraid it would smell strongly in the heat. We eventually bought it at the *pasar* of Rangkasbitung, where it had the additional advantage of being much cheaper than in Djakarta. Japar turned out in a brown sarong and a spotlessly clean white shirt; he was shod in loose leather sandals, and his luggage was confined to a linen bundle, knotted after the fashion of a medieval pilgrim's, and ready to be tied on to a bamboo staff. He was the only member of the trio who could afford to travel light and carefree. The Ministry of Information interpreter was an old friend: Darmono, who had accompanied me through Sumatra on my last visit, and kindly arranged for me to meet tigers. As soon as he heard that I was coming back to Indonesia the poor boy must have guessed that he would soon be on an arduous assignment, although he was courteous enough to assure me that he was delighted to have this opportunity of visiting the jungle and the Baduis—both of which were as novel for him as for me. I must say that Darmono looked the part more than I did; he was extremely elegant in his *safari* outfit, with his slender legs encased in highly polished top boots. We were an oddly assorted little group: Japar, a runaway Badui, Darmono, an urban Javanese, and myself, an inquisitive European. The driver who was taking us to Leuwidamar had instructions to wait there until we returned, whenever that would be. He was not the least bit interested in exploring the jungle.

We were not very lucky with our formal calls on *Bupatis* and other V.I.P.s. At Sanggaran we found the authorities deeply immersed in a weekly conference. Darmono eventually unearthed the *Bupati's* secretary, a young man of great charm, who assured us that no official letter had yet been received from Djakarta, but since we were anxious to arrive at our destination before nightfall he would telephone the *Wedana* of Leuwidamar and instruct him to put us up for the night and give us every assistance.

The palatial residence of the governor of Rangkasbitung farther on was quite deserted so we drove in and out of the grounds in a matter of seconds and made for the *pasar* to buy our salt and fish. Javanese country towns are all planned on the same model; there is little to choose between them. The main buildings, the mosque and the governor's residence with its imposing colonnades, portico and tiled floors, are placed on opposite sides of what could be called the 'green'—if only it were greener. In the centre of this space, which is used for public speeches and demonstrations and thickly planted with stalls on all festive occasions, two banyan trees grow side by side, sometimes protected by a bamboo fence painted in white. These banyan trees are connected with authority—they are also planted outside palaces, and the Javanese are inclined to venerate them. Is this a relic of the Hindu dynasties that ruled over Java in the Middle Ages, a memory of Buddha's Bo-tree of enlightenment, or an archaic survival of animistic tree-worship? Whether one believes in tree-spirits or not, banyan trees attract by their grandfatherly appearance: their trunks are stout with tough arteries running down them; the writhing lianas suspended like wraith's arms from branch to branch give

66

them the air of being mysteriously populated by hordes of spirits, while the splendour of their canopied foliage marks them as aristocrats with long pedigrees behind them.

Beyond Rangkasbitung we left a tolerably good road for an execrable country track pitted with holes; the scenery became wilder and more intense. The land was still cultivated wherever it could be, cut into small careful patterns of rice-fields, but the bamboo forests were thicker and the streams ran less placidly between confused riots of vegetation. There are places in the tropics that were fashioned in a mood of frenzied creation dangerously near the borderline between sanity and madness. This dizzy aspect of nature in Java has seeped into the people's mentality and art-forms. In the course of time, the serene (though exuberant) motifs borrowed from Indian art became distorted by the local idiom, perverted by the strangely passionate mood, the compelling surge of blood to the brain that used to make the quietest of peasants 'run amok' for no apparent reason, and still drives many a modern Javanese to the practice of black magic. People with jungle blood in their veins—Africans and Malays—seem to have the strongest tendencies to deviate from the normal as if possessed by unleashed, unexorcised demons from their ancestral virgin forests.

*   *   *   *

We were driving towards a double range of low, impenetrably wooded hills. Dark clouds were resting on their summits; over-populated Java looked unusually lonely in this region of sinister foreboding. I wondered if the rare one-horned Javan rhinoceros wandered in this neighbourhood. Japar thought not and as far as he knew, no Badui had ever been attacked by a wild beast—but that, said Japar, was probably because the wild creatures knew that the Baduis are a peaceable folk, who hunt infrequently, since they only eat meat three times a year, on the occasion of their feasts. Japar admitted, however, that *we* were in a different position. We were more carnivorous, and our smell must therefore be more aggressive.

In Search of the 'Invisible People'

From time to time, I felt that Japar had private misgivings about the whole trip. He had on several occasions expressed the fear that I would be interfering with the *adat*, or customary law of the Baduis. In spite of Hilman's 'No, no, of course she won't,' Japar's pained flicker of the eyelids plainly indicated that he was unconvinced.

Our arrival at Leuwidamar was not heralded by any form of trumpets—there was no bamboo mat laid down for us, nobody waiting on the *Wedana's* veranda to meet us. We reached this border town at the edge of the jungle a little before five in the afternoon, after a bone-shaking drive. The *Wedana's* house was set far apart from the modest houses of the ordinary citizens. It was built upon a grassy plateau surrounded by magnificent trees. Immediately behind his house, the jungle leaped into vivid life. This is where the motor road ended. There was no electricity, no radio, no newspapers. It was both an end and a beginning. An end to civilization and soft living, and the threshold of a new kind of existence to which we were yet far from adjusted and which, for the next few days, was to be a source of never-ending wonder and novelty.

Darmono left me sitting in a rattan chair upon the veranda while he explored the house in search of the *Wedana*. This gentleman, who was a more than usually reserved type of Javanese, was just getting up from his afternoon siesta. Few visitors ever came to Leuwidamar to interrupt the calm flow of his existence and, moreover, he was quite unprepared for us, because—in spite of the official letter that was supposed to have been sent to him by the Ministry, and despite the promised telephone call from the *Bupati's* secretary at Sanggeran, the *Wedana* had heard nothing about us. He came out to the veranda, shook hands limply after giving me a dark look of suspicion and throwing a scornful glance at Japar, who sat himself upon a bench in the background in a respectful attitude and focused his keen eyes and ears upon Darmono and the *Wedana*, who now entered upon a long, unfruitful dialogue.

When Darmono explained that our intention was to travel into

Badui territory, the *Wedana's* wide mouth curled into a sarcastic smile, accompanied by a vigorous shaking of his round, grey head. He was dead against such an undertaking, but the root of his unco-operative attitude was of a bureaucratic order; he had had no instructions from his superiors. Fortunately he possessed a telephone and Darmono, after some difficulty, succeeded in tracking down the authorities of Sanggeran in their private homes, for it was past office hours, and they assured the *Wedana* that everything was in order with them, with the chiefs in Dja-karta, and with Hilman Djajadiningrat, and we were to be accommodated and helped on our way. The *Wedana* gave in rather half-heartedly, and his wife—a betel-chewing woman with hard, commercial eyes—prepared one of the hottest meals I have ever eaten in Java, with disastrous consequences for me in the middle of the night.

When we had had a much needed bath in conditions of acute discomfort, and were about to sit down to our meal, we discovered that Japar, unseen by anybody in the household, had effected an unobtrusive retreat. What could have happened to him? Where could he have gone? Darmono confided to me that in his opinion Japar had taken offence at the *Wedana's* high-handed manner, for he had not even acknowledged his presence and after all, Japar *was* related to a Badui chief; the *Wedana* appeared to ignore this, and he had spoken all along as if he was in command of the jungle people—and the interpreter of their wishes.

A few minutes later, Japar reappeared in the company of a local acquaintance whom he had brought along to vouch for him and his lineage. This man was more loquacious than Japar and waxed so eloquent on his behalf that the *Wedana* was convinced. He dropped his arrogance and invited Japar to dine with us—Japar was not so easily won over, however; he declined the food, saying that he had already had some in his friend's house, but he accepted a cup of tea and gradually unfroze.

The *Wedana* knew very little, and cared even less, for the Baduis. It was obvious from our conversation, that he regarded them as a bit of a nuisance. The new republic sends up an official every year to take a census and find out what conditions are like —but even he cannot penetrate into the interior. All information about the 'Invisible Ones' is given to him by the 'Blue Baduis' of the outer ring. They do not pay taxes since money is unknown to them—the outer Baduis barter their jungle fruits for the only commodities they accept from the world outside the jungle: unbleached cotton and salt, infrequently a little salted fish. Nobody interferes with them, said the *Wedana*, and they certainly do not interfere with anybody else. Crimes and disputes between them are unknown or at any rate settled quietly among themselves. But Japar told us later that the Muslim villagers of the border territories often encroach upon the Baduis' already limited territory, and that the Baduis repeatedly ask that a 'Bupati with Badui blood should be appointed in Bantam to safeguard Badui interests'.

I asked Japar why he had left his people and when. He hung his head and smiled mischievously before giving me his disarming answer: 'I left when I was twelve—because I wanted to be able to speak to little girls,' he said. Then he explained that according to the severe tribal rules of the 'White Baduis', no male is allowed to address any female outside his family circle. 'Then how do young folk ever get married if they cannot speak to one another?' I asked him. 'Oh, there is plenty of opportunity to meet and see each other working in the fields,' he said. Courtship is bound to be a silent affair, but at least those involved do see each other quite informally and probably over a long period of time, which is more than our Victorian forefathers did, and far more than many orthodox Muslims do even today. But before they are allowed to marry, the young people must seek the consent of the village chief or *pu'un*; but pressure is rarely brought to bear by the parents, and girls, as well as boys, can refuse the match suggested to them by their elders if it is against their wish. No doubt the strict marriage regulations are intended to prevent inbreeding in this already very reduced community.

We rose a little after six and while we ate our breakfast of fried rice, the *Wedana* sent to the village for bearers who would carry our luggage during the first stage of an uphill journey. Japar had exchanged his sarong for a sporty pair of white shorts, on top of which he wore a clean shirt and, on his grey head, the little black Javanese pitchi that resembles a truncated fez. He was barefoot and we soon decided to follow his wise example. 'What about bearers for Japar?' I asked, but our shrewd Badui, lowering his eyes ashamedly, said he believed he could manage without any assistance, in spite of what he had told us in Djakarta. Of course he could, the old rascal! He was in fine fettle and he scaled the blistering hot heights with familiar ease. The jungle had cradled him, and he was in his element. All his talk in front of Hilman about needing bearers to carry him had been sheer nonsense. He was fitter than we were, in spite of his seventy years. And the farther we penetrated into the jungle, the faster the years seemed to roll off him until, in litheness, he was one with the giant lianas and other tentacular denizens of the tropical forest.

Two bearers eventually shambled up to the *Wedana's* house and after a puzzled look at our luggage began to tie it up with unusual inefficiency. After a while, they decided that they would require more rope, and so the youngest member of the team was sent back into the village. It took him over half an hour to find a ragged piece of rope a yard long. Finally, after a lot of tying, un-tying, and rearranging, our varied pieces of baggage were firmly bound to the ends of two bamboo poles which our bearers hoisted on to their shoulders with some effort, for the loads were heavy. They wanted ten rupiahs each, they said, to walk up to Tjikan-geri, our first halting-place.

The *Wedana* extended a flabby hand, like a tired frog, and his wife stood beside him, nodding and parting her lips in a betel-red smile. We walked round the house and up a narrow path. In less than five minutes we were engulfed by the jungle. It had been raining, and this made progress more difficult. Bare toes used as crampons—once you become used to manœuvring these neglected appendages—are vastly superior to anything manufac-tured, but oh how we wobbled when crossing the many bridges

71

of bamboo trunks thrown across deep ravines! With or without shoes, it was a terrifying experience; wet bamboo trunks have a nasty way of revolving upon themselves, and naturally there was no such thing as a rail to hold on to. Japar and the bearers tackled these bridges gracefully, but my inch by inch, unsteady advance must have looked comic; I was, however, fearfully conscious all the time that it *could* have been tragic. One false step and—it was a long, long way down to the bottom where mountain streams snarled between unfriendly rocks. Japar and the bearers marched on, never casting a look behind them. Both Darmono and I were very anxious to live, and only the instinct of survival kept us on our unreliable feet. By the end of our first day in the jungle, however, we had improved to the point of being able to relax and enjoy the scenery. The first few strenuous hours, however, were too painful and nerve-racking to allow for an appreciation of our surroundings. I felt as if I were climbing through red treacle, with frequent jabs from jutting stones, but this and the heat were tolerable compared to the recurrent nightmare of bamboo bridges.

When we reached the crest of the hill, after a long and preoccupied lapse of time, we paused for breath and had a good look around us. It was not quite so hot up here, and the forest had given way to untidy rows of tall alang-alang grass over the tops of which I could see rolling hills on each side that merged into still more hills in the distance. Japar pointed to a cone that stood out from the surrounding ranges. 'That is the sacred hill of the Baduis,' he said, 'that is where the *Artjas Domas* is to be found.' He had never been there himself; he had only heard about it from his father who used to accompany the other chiefs there every year for the simple rites among the moss, the stones, and the sacred trees that represent human beings and bear mysterious traces of their joys and sufferings upon their trunks and branches. It is there they gather the moss and white sand which is taken down to the *Bupati* every year as a mark of homage.

After an easy walk of about a mile along the top of the hills, we plunged into another forest, lighter than the first we had crossed, which had been as dark as a tunnel and almost as silent. Here were shrubs of mauve blossoms, and a tree of golden flowers humming with wild bees; there must have been millions of them, and if the bearers had not been so far away with my luggage so securely tied to a bamboo pole, I would have stopped to record this remarkable bee symphony. Moonlight orchids trailed from many a tree-trunk like offerings to sylvan gods; butterflies— striped black and white, or patterned in brown and cream like *batik* sarongs and splotched with bright orange circles—fluttered across our path.

From time to time a group of peasants passed us, after asking where we came from and where we were going. They carried bananas or coffee beans, for sale in the *pasar* of Leuwidamar. Then two more came along, wearing blue sarongs and a blue turban. 'Baduis!' I exclaimed excitedly. Japar nodded. 'Yes,' he said, 'they are Blue Baduis from one of the outer villages.' I looked at them with undisguised curiosity. They too were carry- ing fruit but they did not hail us to ask questions as the others had done and after one astonished glance at me, they became quite shy, and lowered their large, velvety eyes like timid gazelles. They were of a different build from the other Javanese peasants —these strange, wild men in blue; they were stockier and stur- dier, and their faces were of a heavier cast but, as I discovered later, there are many types among the Baduis. 'How aloof they are!' I remarked. 'They walk like a people whose destiny is apart from that of other mortals.' Japar laughed. He had be- come more communicative since we had entered the jungle. 'They certainly believe they are a people apart,' he said. 'Their timid looks are part of the *adat*, but at heart, they are extremely proud. They believe that Batarratunggal, their first god and ruler, will come down to earth again to govern the Baduis and the world. The present Badui leaders are his descendants—the wise men of the villages know all this and keep the records.'

'But I thought they didn't know how to write,' I objected. Japar looked mysterious. 'That is true for the bulk of the Baduis, but the wise ones have their own way of writing—their signs, that are not like anyone else's. Only they can read and interpret them.'

'And is it true, Japar, that the Baduis can foretell the future?'

Japar nodded gravely. 'The priests can, after they have fasted and spent many hours meditating. Then they speak silently,' he said. What he meant by the apparent contradiction 'speaking silently', we could not find out. Did it signify that the priests, in a trance-state after prolonged mental and physical preparation, are able to converse with spirits? Japar did not seem very sure what to say on this subject, but he went on to tell us that the Baduis had predicted the world war, and many other events that had eventually come to pass.

'The *Artjas Domas* shows them what is happening in the world,' Japar added as an afterthought. 'They can see it all up there without having to come down and read the newspapers! But they only go up there once a year,' he laughed. 'Because the signs that the priests see there are not about little things—they are concerned only with important changes, things that go deep into people's hearts and lives.'

'Didn't you ever think of becoming a priest?' I asked him jocularly.

'Oh no,' Japar replied, quite seriously. 'I could never have been one—the "power" is handed down from father to son.'

'And when you go back to see your people—do they ask you questions about the world outside? Are they interested?'

'Yes, they are. They want to know if people are well-governed and happy. Of course they don't really believe that anything can go well outside, since other people don't follow Badui laws!'

'And what about you, Japar? Don't your people ever try to make you stay with them again?'

Japar shook his head and smiled evasively. 'I have been exiled, because I refused to accept their laws. I could never live there again, even if I wanted to. That is the law. But as I am a *pu'un's* (chief's) son, I am allowed to spend three days among the inner people every year. At the end of the third day, I must go. And I am not permitted to take part in their celebrations, or go to the

Artjas Domas—I am an outlaw, but I am still a Badui,' he explained.

On the whole, it sounded like a fairly tolerant code—not at all what one would expect from a jungle people. But then nobody could be less savage than the peaceful Baduis. They could argue that *we* are the savages, with our tanks and our guns and our guided missiles. Who knows, maybe they will inherit the earth when we have smouldered away in radio-active dust!

We paused in an avenue of trees, tall as the Perpendicular columns of an English cathedral, taller than those of Beauvais that finally collapsed when the architect's vision had surpassed his technique. The branches above us spread like fan ribs against the vault of the sky. We sat on a mossy bank and lowered our voices, as if we had entered a place of worship. It was without doubt an appropriate place for worship: calm, cool, and majestic. We had a choir, too; deep-throated tropical birds intoning grave, contralto melodies. This was the jungle's other face, its lesser known, contemplative face when, suddenly tiring of exuberance, it pulls itself up and stretches to the heavens, inviting all those who wander through to raise their thoughts to infinity; perhaps not so much their thoughts as their feelings, for in the jungle you feel through all your pores, so strongly that sometimes you believe that you are seeing and smelling with your pores too. We Europeans ignore this in our dealings with jungle peoples. We don't realize how their environment makes them *feel* rather than think, clearly.

Emerging again into the open, we began to feel terribly thirsty. 'There don't seem to be any streams here,' I complained, looking over the edge of the hill. 'When you are thirsty in the jungle, you must look up, not down!' laughed Japar, stopping under a coconut tree. He made a sign to one of our bearers who immediately drew out the lethal-looking axe or *parang* which every Javanese peasant carries at his belt for the purpose of hacking down coconuts and firewood. Our bearer walked up a tree, making good use of his flexible toes; it looked stupidly simple.

When the bearer came streaking down from the tree, he cut a

neat round hole out of the centre of two coconuts and presented them to us saying that *he* felt hungry and fancied a couple of salty fish from our offering for the Baduis. We let him have his way —he was evidently determined to have it anyway, and he pulled out two fish by their tails and munched them with relish. The sourish coconut juice was tepid, but plentiful—almost a quart I should think in my coconut—and the sensation of so much liquid passing down one's throat had a refreshing though purely temporary effect.

We came to the jungle village of Tjikangeri just after noon. It was as quiet as a beehive whose inmates are out gathering honey. Japar led us to the village headman's house, built on a hill overlooking the glaucous village pond, which also served as a communal bathroom. The headman's house was carefully shut and looked like a neat bamboo box. There was no garden attached to it, but a wide, well-swept path. A thin, friendly little mongrel advanced wagging its tail, as if to make up for the absence of human greetings; in the thicket of bamboo and banana trees and palms that led from the house down to the main track through the village, a gay-plumed cock and his scraggy wives scratched unconcernedly among the shady undergrowth.

Opposite the veranda stood a smaller bamboo building in the centre of which hung a large oval drum with a stick beside it. Newcomers are expected to announce their arrival by beating upon this drum; our bearers performed this task as soon as they had deposed our luggage in the shady interior, which was occupied by two bunks and a bench. The hollow sound of the drum hit the coconut palms one by one, whirring through and out of the village as if a carrier-pigeon had been released. Our bearers now demanded more salt fish—they were insatiable. 'No—you have had enough—this is a present,' I said, but they only laughed, peered into the basket, and pulled out a couple of fish each, which they chewed up, tails and all, before pocketing their rupiahs and going back to Leuwidamar.

It was too hot to move, so I sat underneath a coconut palm to wait for the headman to appear, but nobody came. The drum was impressive to look at, but it was quite ineffective. 'The men must be working in the rice-fields,' said Japar ruefully. 'Until what time do they usually stay there? Don't they come home for lunch?' I asked. Japar shook his head sadly. 'They work until about two or three in the afternoon, and they have a meal soon after that,' he said, 'but sometimes the headman returns to offer hospitality to passing travellers when he hears the drum. Perhaps they didn't strike it loud enough,' and he advanced to beat it several times in quick succession until it roared like a bad-tempered lion. By this time we were all very hungry but I for one did not fancy more coconut. Very generously, Darmono unwrapped the large parcel of provisions which his newly-wedded wife had prepared for him, and extracted several packets of 'sticky' rice, and hard-boiled eggs with pale green shells: 'salted eggs', he called them, and so they were, with a vengeance. Despite my hunger, I simply could not swallow them. Japar wandered off to explore the village, returning five minutes later to inform us that only women and children were to be seen and two men known as *orang-rondas* whose duty it is to watch over the village and guard the womenfolk during the working-hours when the rest of the male population is away. These men are also used as messengers and bearers, but they could do nothing for us until they had received formal instructions from the village head.

Another couple of travellers arrived an hour after us; they struck the visitor's drum with the same lack of response, and then stretched out on the bunks inside the 'waiting-room', where Japar was prostrating himself in prayer. (I wondered whether he dared to do this before his Badui relatives.)

These travellers were a brisk young man who walked barefoot but was carrying a brand new pair of army boots over his shoulder, and his wife. From the loud tone of their voices, so different from the low, refined accent of the Central Javanese, it was obvious that they were both from West Java.

At three o'clock in the afternoon, the village sprung to life as the field-workers came back, their faces shaded by wide coolie hats, with baskets of fruit and vegetables suspended from bamboo

77

poles; the headman's house opened up, and his wife came out on the veranda to ask us up for tea. The headman did not present himself until he had taken his bath in the pond and changed into a clean shirt and sarong. Then he stepped forward, wearing the little black pitchi that gives the Javanese a kind of bowler-hatted status, to inquire what he could do for us. After listening gravely to Darmono's explanations, he declared that we would have to spend the night in his house, because it was now too late to arrange for bearers to accompany us as far as the next village, but these would be laid on early next morning.

In the meantime, he said, we were welcome to share the little he had. We started off with the tea, which his wife had poured into little white cups (saucers were deemed unnecessary) on the bamboo mat round which we, and any other visitors who might drop in, were expected to squat. Before being admitted to the tea-drinking circle, we complied with local civilities by making sure our toes were free from dust. For this purpose we were handed a strange-looking object which I feel sure would stump the distinguished members of the 'Animal, mineral or vegetable?' panel. It consisted of a broad, hollow bamboo tube filled with water and provided with a stopper at each end. Guests sit on the steps of the veranda, extend their feet, and sprinkle their toes with the water from this tube before stepping inside. It does not matter if your feet are wet, so long as they are clean.

Darmono watched the tea being poured out and bent over to murmur anxiously in my ear: 'Do you think we should drink this tea? It's pretty obvious where the water came from—there's only one source of supply for the whole village, and that is the pond in which everybody bathes and you know what else.' 'Are you sure?' I queried, looking at the light amber-coloured liquid that filled my cup. It looked clear and innocent enough. 'Absolutely, that's the way in most of the villages of the interior. There just isn't anywhere else for the water to come from. What do you think we should do?'

'The best thing,' I declared, 'is *not* to think about it. If we do, we shall be bound to get ill. From now on, I refuse to believe in germs. How can we refuse our hosts? They would be offended and I must say I'm extremely thirsty.'

'Well, I suppose the water will have been boiled,' said Darmono, peering doubtfully into his cup. 'It *looks* all right—funny, isn't it, because the pond-water . . .' 'Yes, I know,' I interrupted hastily; I did not want to remember what the pond-water looked like, 'but now we're in the jungle, we'd better make up our minds to live like the jungle folk.'

'Some things take getting used to,' sighed Darmono.

What *I* found less easy to get used to was the communal bathroom—that is, the dark end of the pond to which a muddy path descended between banana trees, where a landing-stage (it looked more like a diving-board to me) of slippery bamboo poles had been flung across the pond and provided with a row of pierced coconut shells that served as dippers. After some hesitation, I made my way down a little before dusk with my plastic toilet bag and a towel over my arm. The bamboos were wet and it was all I could do to prevent myself from tumbling into the pond. At least I had the satisfaction of being alone, for the healthy-minded villagers think nothing of sharing a corner of the 'bathroom' with a neighbour—of the same or of the opposite sex. In the latter event, each one of the two modestly turns his or her back on the other and both proceed unconcernedly with their ablutions. Once you have got the hang of it, I suppose it is a fairly easy matter to wind and unwind a sarong without exposing over-much of one's anatomy—but a button-through dress, bra, and panties inevitably involve a strip-tease, and I found it difficult to disrobe inconspicuously. People kept wandering about between the trees round the pond and I knew that at any moment I would be obliged to move over for a newcomer. In the end, I contented myself with a series of half-hearted dabs under my dress. I couldn't think *how* to wash my back without uncovering myself completely. Brushing my teeth presented other problems of a minor nature—there was of course no such thing as a tooth glass (the perforated coconut shell was more than useless) so I was obliged to further pollute the pond water with chalky traces of tooth powder. It was altogether a most uncomfortable experience.

The last meal of the day was served before six and one had to be genuinely hungry to eat it. Boiled rice, yams, and a sourish creamy substance called *tempé*, made from fermented yam, filled us but did not satisfy our craving for some kind of flavour. Nor was there anything that could be chewed. Every item on the drab menu was soft and mealy. Perhaps that is why most of the people have such bad teeth.

The headman and his wife ate their meal a couple of yards away from us, off the same bamboo mat. We were given a plate each, and a fork of the kind supplied by British railway station buffets. This was a luxury. Personally, however, I prefer my own fingers to a smelly tin fork. A narrow strip of a room, bare except for a thin mattress laid on the floor, was allotted to me for my sleeping compartment (Darmono and Japar slept in the 'dining-room').

These too were luxuries that I would henceforth have to forgo: a place to myself and a mattress, which lay like a shroud in the light of the coconut-oil lamp flickering like a funeral taper at its foot.

There was nowhere to hang my clothes, so I wrapped them into a neat Girl Guide-like bundle beside my toilet bag. Fortunately I am not in the habit of rising during the night, or I should have been in a predicament—with two doors to open and two bodies to walk over before being able to reach the dark, bleak, exterior. . . .

I retired to my compartment early, shut the fragile bamboo door, and blew out the light, for it was too dim to be able to read or write by. Next door, and very audible through the thin partition, the headman and his visitors continued to talk and smoke clove-scented *kretek* cigarettes until midnight. A muffled sound of drums stumbled up from the village—it sounded like the accompaniment of *penchak* exercises alternating with the rhythmic rise and fall of Muslim prayers. I lay awake for a long time listening to these unfamiliar sounds from the depths of my bamboo basket of a bedroom. Although I could not under-

how difficult his people were. His lean figure soon passed out of sight between the trees of his homeland; we walked slowly back and began to explore the village to pass the time until his return but my thoughts were in the hills, with the forest folk. What would their reaction be? The hours dragged by.

The frontier village was built in the haphazard way of most jungle-forest settlements; some of the houses were built on a minute, well-swept plateau, others formed a neighbourly little square, while the most independent turned to overlook the forest which formed a natural barrier on every side. We discovered a duck-pond in the hollow; most of the villagers owned hens, ducks, and Muscovy ducks. They were too poor to afford water buffaloes. In the little village hall we came upon a group of agile youngsters practising *penchak* under the guidance of a wizened old teacher who entertained us with a cleverly mimed monkey-dance which sent us into peals of laughter.

The children were on holiday, but the local school-teacher was keeping them usefully busy by employing them to hoe the plot of land round the tiny schoolhouse. They worked with gusto and laughed merrily when I brought down my tape recorder to record their childish conversation—all except one tiny tot who took fright when the inscrutable black microphone was held close to her little baked apple of a face, and burst out crying. It is not often that one hears a Javanese child crying. This outburst in front of the strange new machine subsided, however, as soon as it was whisked out of sight, when the little girl gravely proceeded to dip her minute sarong into a muddy puddle and to wring it out, as she had seen her mother do by the village pond. I was so absorbed watching the naked tot with her pouting face 'washing' out her only sarong that I didn't even think of taking a picture! Now, as I see her in my mind's eye, I deeply regret my negligence, for she was such a cuddly subject and her baby-Eve figure was delightful. But I console myself with the reflection that my camera would probably have frightened her as much as the microphone. I attempted to film the village children later, but their interest in my cine-camera reduced them to an immobile unphotogenic fascination. They sat like worried sparrows on the high verandas of their houses, with their feet dangling in mid-air and hardly the flicker of a smile on their usually bright faces.

I was glad that I had set up the cine-camera outside the headman's house—although I did not expect the results to be too good in the dim light that filtered through the coconut palms. I was fortunate to catch some of the Baduis unawares. They were Blue Baduis, members of the outer community, who own land at the end of the frontier village; a file of these Baduis, men and women, passed through the village morning and evening to cut and collect firewood from their property. The first intimation I had of their presence was an excited whisper from one of the Muslim villagers. 'Here come the Baduis!' he exclaimed, as if it were a novel sight for him, and I turned my camera on them just in time. I was a little surprised to discover that the Baduis are held in awe by the villagers—probably because they lead different lives, because so little is known about them, and because they hold themselves aloof from other people. Maybe the villagers believe that the Baduis possess a magic power that keeps intruders away; but it is strange to find a feeling almost amounting to fear among people who see them every day and who live at the foot of their territory. It is true that the 'white' or 'invisible' Baduis are almost as much of an anachronistic mystery to them as they are to us who live nine thousand miles away.

The Baduis advanced in single file with heads held high. All of them, even the women, wore indigo blue turbans. One old woman with pendulous withered breasts was naked to the waist, but the younger ones wore blue sarongs wound round their armpits. Most of them carried flat baskets and they made straight for their destination with hardly a glance to the right or to the left. No doubt it is against their *adat* to stare or take an interest in strangers. They are indeed a people apart, I thought, as I peered into the viewfinder and pressed the starter. They had never seen a camera before, and they had never been filmed. It was an historical occasion, of which they were completely oblivious; they walked past me haughtily, without even noticing the camera.

84

Such a total lack of curiosity is really phenomenal. I, on the contrary, could not take my eyes off them. Not that they were handsome to look at, rather the reverse; most of them had heavy, scowling faces, and the low foreheads peculiar to so many aboriginals. But it is impossible to generalize about them. Some of them, for instance, have the same lanky, straight hair as the Javanese, while others have wavy and even curly hair. Most of the men wear it long and twisted into a plait folded into their turban. One young woman was carrying her naked babe to the fields astride her hip, in the Javanese way. The old woman with the lined face and grey hair was far taller than the rest; but in general their stature is more or less the same—perhaps slightly inferior—as that of the non-Badui jungle communities. Altogether, they are not what one expects from the jungle. This solemn procession of silent, unsmiling men and women, all dressed exactly alike, and totally absorbed by their manual labours, looked more like a gang of convicts on hard labour. I smiled to think how many people at home believe jungle people's life to be a pagan paradise of freedom from restraint, moral and otherwise: wild orgies on palm wine and sexual licence accompanied by a hysterical beating of drums. The Baduis, who couldn't be more primitive from a mental or material standpoint, are in fact more puritanical and certainly more virtuous than were Cromwell's men! It is strange to think that a community of almost monastic severity grows in these forests like a rare species of wild flower, uncultivated and tenacious.

The villagers stood and stared after the Baduis at a respectful distance, with the rapt attention of small children at the zoo. Nobody advanced to speak to them. It is evidently an accepted fact that the Baduis have no desire to be sociable. I cannot remember having seen anything more extraordinary in human relationships than this confrontation of peoples living practically side by side as complete strangers; this is possibly the smallest, and most impenetrable of all the 'curtains'—bamboo or iron—that divide our suspicious world.

*   *   *   *

Just before sunset, Japar came back triumphantly, accompanied by a Blue Badui whom he introduced as the *pu'un* of one of the outer villages; he wished to make our acquaintance and conduct a preliminary discussion. He was an open-faced, jaunty fellow, this *pu'un*, not a bit like his severe kinsmen whom we had seen passing through the village; he had black teeth and smiling eyes, and he looked at me with friendly curiosity as we squatted on the veranda. 'I have sent word to the three *pu'uns* of the inner community,' he told us, 'asking them, if they agree, to come and meet you here tomorrow morning. I don't know what they will do.' He shrugged his shoulders and turned towards Japar whose eyes were glinting like a ferret's. 'We've never had a similar request before. They may not come.' His eyes roved round the headman's 'parlour' and paused to examine my tape recorder and camera. Then he stopped chewing betel-nut to point at these products of our machine civilization and to warn me: 'On no account must you use these. Japar has told me about them. It is not allowed by our laws. They must be hidden and you must promise not to bring them out if the White Baduis come.' I was bitterly disappointed but I had no choice. I promised that I would neither record nor film the Baduis (I consoled myself a little with the knowledge that I had *some* film in the can already. How fortunate that the Baduis had passed that way before I had been bound to a promise!)

Japar accompanied the Blue Badui to the boundary line to see him off. He bid us good night jovially enough and said he hoped to see us again the next day, but he had refused to share any refreshment with us. '*Tidah boleh*'—it is not allowed, he said with a laugh as if even he thought it was a huge joke; nevertheless he kept strictly to the rules.

Soon after he left we heard the evening prayers being chanted in the *langgar* or prayer-house, a little way down the 'road'. I slipped down to watch them through the open door. The women were squatting on the right and the men on the left, with their faces turned towards the west where Mecca, the Muslim's second capital, lies. Night had swooped upon us like the wings of an owl over its unsuspecting prey; coconut-oil lamps set in white saucers sent up timid tongues of flame between the silhouettes of the villagers at prayer. They had almost finished. . . . Was it permitted to record them or would my infidel intrusion be resented? By no means, on the contrary—and the brisk little man who was leading the prayers started them up all over again for my special benefit, so that I could push my inquisitive microphone through the bamboo opening. Several sleek heads swerved round, forgetting Mecca for an instant, to look at the strange machine.

It rained sharply all through the night as though the heavens were shooting bamboo arrows at us from millions of bows; the damp air rose from the sodden ground through the bamboo floorboards. I shivered in my corner and longed for a blanket, and a mattress, and the dawn which was so long in coming.

People seemed to eat even less here than in Chiboleger. Weak tea and boiled rice was put down before us for breakfast about 7 a.m., and a repetition of this, which served as lunch, appeared again at 2 p.m. with the addition of a new vegetable of almond-like consistency that tasted like sour raw potato. No villager ever eats more than two meals a day. We felt hungry (I just could *not* stuff myself with plain boiled rice) and were delighted when a little golden girl appeared under a wide coolie hat selling *koué*, or crisp rice-cakes, and *chu-chur* made from palm sugar. We bought all she had and she leant against the veranda and laughed to see how quickly we disposed of her morning's work. Although she looked so young, she told us that she was already married.

When nine o'clock came and there was still no sign of the Invisible Ones, my heart began to sink. Surely the jungle folk, who are early risers, would have come by now if they meant to see us? Well, I had been warned! Nobody had believed in the success of my expedition except myself, and that belief was fast proving to be a delusion. Even so, it was better to have had faith and be disappointed than not to have come at all. I glanced up at the tantalizing hill-path leading to the forbidden territory. 'I am afraid they have decided not to come,' I exclaimed sadly. Japar had begun to show signs of impatience too and he looked up at the path, pursing his lips. Then, without saying a word, he strode forward. 'Where are you going?' Darmono asked him. 'I'm going to find out what is happening,' said Japar determinedly. Well, it was good of him to try, I thought, but how much influence did he really have with his people? As he had admitted, he was a renegade who could not stay for more than three days in his jealously guarded homeland. Would his people consent to forgo their sacred *adat* on the strength of an indirect request from Hilman, who was no longer the *Bupati* of Bantam?

It began to rain angrily while we waited in the muddy main street to waylay more Blue Baduis. A small group of them came out of the forest and took shelter on a deserted veranda before returning to their territory. 'Let's go and speak to them,' I said to Darmono, and we sauntered down casually, in case they took fright and moved off. There were two women and a boy who might have been eighteen or twenty. The women turned their faces away as we approached, probably because of Darmono's presence, but the boy, who was sitting cross-legged beside a little bamboo bird-trap in which he had just caught a jungle songster, was too full of curiosity to move. He spoke a few words of Indonesian, unlike many other Baduis who only know their own archaic form of Sundanese. While the Badui boy answered Darmono's questions, in shy monosyllables, he looked at me spellbound. It was obvious that he had never seen human beings with light eyes before, and he could not take his eyes away from mine. It was a strange sensation, because he did not look at me as if I were a fellow human being but rather as if I had been some rare jungle creature whom he would have liked to capture and keep as a pet. His eyes stalked mine with the eagerness of a hunter. I once had a Persian cat that used to follow the movements of my eyes when I was reading with a similar intensity before she finally pounced upon them. As I looked into the sloe-black eyes of the Badui, I realized that his too were different from any other eyes I had ever seen—they had a quality about them that was not quite human, but this was probably because they were accustomed to looking at a different kind of world from mine.

This Badui, unlike most of his people, was almost handsome. He had a full face, a large firm mouth and a gentle smile; his folded limbs were rounded and supple. He was the perfect epitome of the 'Noble Savage'. After a few minutes' conversation, he shook himself and said he must be going. The women had suggested this to him before, because the rain had stopped and they seemed anxious to be on their way. The youth uncoiled himself with serpentine grace, picked up his bird-trap, and walked away. His stock of jungle lore must be enormous I thought as I watched him go; what a joy he would be to ethnographers—and to Boy Scouts! The little Javanese with the new pair of army boots whom we had met at Tjikangeri suddenly appeared before us, accompanied by his loud-spoken wife. 'Been talking with the Tarzans?' he asked us with an amused look in the direction of the departing Baduis. 'Their women are not very pretty,' said his wife, smoothing her sleek black hair. 'Strange folk altogether,' her husband remarked thoughtfully. 'Did you ever hear óf anybody else who wanted the world to remain just as it was on the day Adam was created!' And he laughed sarcastically.

We walked back slowly to the headman's house, and I raised my eyes despondently to the jungle track which we had nicknamed 'the road to Eden'. Then I stopped, hardly daring to believe my eyes. 'Look, Darmono,' I gasped, 'the White Ones—the Invisible People—they are coming after all!' It was true. For the first time in their long history, the Invisible People had consented to come down from their jungle stronghold to meet a white woman. The Blue Badui *pu'un* led the unique little procession; behind him, in single file, walked the *pu'uns* of the three villages of the interior, easily recognizable in their unbleached turbans and sarongs; Japar jubilantly brought up the rear. The White Baduis advanced at a measured pace—they carried staffs and looked as dignified as three kings, supremely conscious of the fact that they are the descendants of Batarratunggal and the faithful guardians of his austere laws until he comes again to find his people and rule the earth. Unlike the rest of humanity, they will have waited in peace, unshaken in their attachment to non-violence.

I was itching to be able to film this rare encounter in the middle of the jungle, but I had given my word, and they on their side were making an unheard of concession to please Hilman, their kinsman in the far-off capital, who has Badui blood in his veins and is an heir of Batarratunggal's kingdom. Darmono and I advanced to meet them. The Blue Badui smiled brightly, but he was a little more on his dignity than the day before. The presence of the superior White Ones evidently had to be marked by a due amount of respect. We invited them to come and sit on the veranda, but this was apparently *tidah boleh* and against the *adat* of the White Ones, who gravely squatted on the ground in front of the headman's house. The Blue *pu'un*, however, sat with us and served as an interpreter. The White Ones, who are not allowed to address any women outside the family circle, lowered their eyes in front of me like bashful monks, while I unashamedly devoured them with my eyes. By this time the entire village had assembled round the house, for the advent of the Invisible Ones was an even greater attraction than the arrival of a European female. The White Ones sat unperturbed, with their staffs at their feet—grave, aloof but fundamentally at ease. They were very dissimilar in type. The youngest could have been in his twenties; he was smooth-skinned, with staring eyes set wide apart —Tibetan eyes—and a square jaw. The second *pu'un* had a low forehead and a sallow, grooved face, but the third and eldest, who is reputed to be a saint and a sage, was a benevolent old gentleman who, in other clothes, would pass unnoticed in an English crowd, for he had a very light complexion, a narrow face, and the gentle bearing of a civilized person. There was nothing of the jungle-hunter about *him*, and he was obviously of a superior caste to the others. A stone image of him placed in the portal of a European cathedral would not have looked out of place. Still, I had not expected to find a sage and I was a little taken aback. I even thought I had seen his face before somewhere—I remembered afterwards that I had seen it in the cloister of Pamplona Cathedral, in Spanish Navarre. (This was the second connection I had found between the Baduis and the sculpture of a Pyrenean country.) It was the face of Job, as portrayed on one of the Romanesque capitals there: patient, long-suffering, resigned, and tempered by a long inward struggle. It was not a face to be easily forgotten.

We had a strange conversation, through two interpreters: Darmono and the Blue *pu'un*. The White Ones were not anxious to answer questions, and their replies were brief. They told us that their numbers have dwindled to less than two thousand people living in twenty-two villages (including the forty families of the three inner or White Ones' villages). They only cultivate dry rice-fields and eat meat once a year. Their daily fare consists of rice, vegetables, eggs, wild honey, and coconuts. The whole village fasts once a month and every time there is a circumcision ceremony; the Baduis are monogamous and the White Ones are so strict that they not only refrain from smoking but are not even allowed to chew betel-nuts (as the Blue Baduis do). They believe in immortality, and in reincarnation like the Hindus—and in a purgatory through which souls are made to walk on a 'line of steel points' through an avenue of flames.

From what we gathered, the Baduis have no day of rest and they work without the help of domesticated animals. 'Is it then forbidden to have four-footed animals?' I asked. They shook their heads sadly. 'We had water buffaloes once,' they said, 'but the Muslims stole them from us.' It seems that the Baduis had retired into their forests before the enemy and when they re-emerged, all their buffaloes had gone! Their peaceful laws being what they are, they could not take any retaliatory action and so ever since they have been without any four-footed animals (except for dogs and cats which they keep as pets). When I asked them to sum up their moral code, they replied succinctly: 'It is forbidden to us to hurt other people by way of mouth, eyes, hands, or feelings.' (The Ten Commandments in a nutshell.)

Japar told us afterwards, with a malicious chuckle, that he had invoked this code as an argument to persuade the White Ones to come to see us. Apparently they had been most unwilling to depart from their *adat* and Japar had had to use all his powers of persuasion. 'Hilman wants you to do this for him, and if you don't you'll pass for an unfriendly people,' he had told them— and the Baduis, who do not wish to hurt people's feelings, had at last agreed to reveal their faces, to prove that it is not misanthropy that makes them prefer their jungle solitudes.

When the time came to offer our present of salt and fish the Baduis said they could only accept it if it came from Hilman— and they proudly made it clear that they would not take the gift in return for anything they had said!

They waited until we were ready to go. Perhaps that was another rule of their jungle etiquette—*they* were the hosts, and *we* were the guests. As we made ready to leave, the Blue *pu'un* whispered to me: 'Some of us will be going down to play our bamboo instruments at Leuwidamar for the Independence Day celebrations of August 17th. If you want to use your machines then, it will be quite all right, for our Gods do not rule over *that* territory. Up here they would certainly object—but not down there.' This was good news. 'I shall be there,' I said, and then I added as an afterthought: 'So you know about President Sukarno and independence?' The Blue Badui laughed. 'Of course. Our people'—and he looked at the White Ones—'told us long ago that we would have independence under the rule of the crescent when the white men would go home. *We* knew long before you did!'

He waved us a bright good-bye, the bearers made off and I took a long last look at the Invisible People. They were gravely studying the ground at their feet. Yet they had come—and they must have walked many miles. I hope that they enjoyed the fish, which I was relieved to give away. They did not even say good-bye to Japar, but he did not appear to be upset by their undemonstrativeness. No Javanese ever shows any outward signs of affection. I would have liked to shake hands with the saintly old *pu'un*, but that was quite impossible. We stole away, barefoot. I still could not quite believe that I was the first white woman to have set eyes on the Invisible People.

✳   ✳   ✳   ✳

'It's really amazing,' commented Darmono as we struggled to follow our quick-stepping bearers downhill through the deserted village and along the edge of the rice-fields, 'to think that such unprogressive people should still be wandering around in our Republic!' He sounded resentful. 'Unprogressive and everlasting, uncannily able to enter into the essence of things . . . at least they have come to terms with their world and are untroubled,' I remarked, but Darmono mumbled on to himself unheeding. As the editor of an Economic News Bulletin designed to impress his countrymen with the facts of modern business and industry, he was far from taking my romantic view of the Baduis. Whereas I felt refreshed, he could only feel pained.

Our philosophical reflections were soon cut short, however, because the sticky descent required concentration. Our bearers, who seemed to be engaged in a cross-country run, had disappeared from view. Perhaps if one were to imitate their jerky, shuffling gait progress would be easier; after all there is a great deal to be said in favour of the platitudinous: 'When you are in Rome, do as the Romans do.' Upon second thoughts, however, I decided that this was not the time to experiment. Better keep to my own uncertain, wary way of placing my feet in the squelching mud than emulate the bold tread of those who had been bred in the jungle. Darmono struggled and slipped, struggled and slipped in his *shikari* leggings. All too frequently we sank ankle-deep in the red mire that sucked us in with an ecstatic gurgle. We were returning by another route to a kampong called Tjisimut on the banks of a river which we could hear in the far distance although we could not yet see it. We were altogether in a very watery landscape, and constantly flanked by terraced cascades of wet paddy-fields, not unlike a utilitarian Versailles. How effective they would look under flood-lighting, with the vivid green of the coconut palms and giant curved ferns scribbling extravagant designs in the background! The Javanese were only imitating nature at their doorstep when they devised the rounded characters of their alphabet. There was no rice in the fields now; most of them were choked with pink and golden weeds and vibrating with the songs of tuneful frogs. I cannot bring myself to use so disparaging a word as 'croak' for the melodious sound made by Javanese frogs; for a long time I was under the impression that I was listening to birds.

The rains had melted the ridges between the rice-fields and we paddled through them, weary of so much water and heat from the grey sky toppling overhead in its menacing, equatorial way. It was always on the point of crushing us, yet we survived, panting with the strain of having to constantly pull our legs out of the slush. The slow progress of Everest climbers at oxygen-less altitudes had nothing on our tortoise-paced tropical march back to civilization. At last we reached the topaz-coloured river and staggered beside its sliding, lacy wavelets—for it was in an impetuous mood—all the way to Tjisimut. Flowers had been planted in front of the houses in this village—a rare sight in Java where peasants prefer to leave blossoms to entwine trees or decorate cemeteries.

It was a Friday and the men were chanting verses from the Koran in a very new mosque with whitewashed walls and an onion-shaped aluminium cupola built on the river bank. A straggling procession of people balancing trays of fruit on their heads were crossing the river, swaying a little when they reached the middle where the current was strongest. Most of these jungle rivers are shallow and there are no bridges. What happens in the swollen rainy season I do not know. Probably everybody just stays at home and waits with Asiatic patience and Islamic fatalism until the floods subside.

Darmono sat on the bank and tugged at his beautiful *shikari* leggings while the village children gathered round and chuckled; he soon enlisted their aid, however, and had them pulling for all they were worth, with a line of helpers clasping waists behind until the boots came off at last amid shrieks of laughter as the children tumbled over each other. One of the tots even rolled into the river, but he soon picked himself up and was out again—wet but warm. Our bearers waited on the opposite side, from where they watched us wading across with impassive faces. I paused in

94

midstream, to enjoy the sensation of the hot rushing water against and between my toes. A little farther on we sank into a deep pool and felt the river's tight embrace about our waists. We had deviated from the course which the peasants knew so well, but neither of us wanted to have to swim because of our various impedimenta; I was holding shoes and a camera, while Darmono was carrying his precious leggings.

Our bearers had assured us that we could take a bus from Tjisimut to Leuwidamar for, contrary to what was indicated on the maps we had consulted before our departure, there *was* a road between the two localities. It was a road better suited to jeeps than motor-cars as we soon discovered when we walked up to the solitary garage on the opposite shore, where two harassed mechanics were disembowelling the one and only bus. It was only just recognizable as a bus, for its wheels had been removed. We looked at these amputated objects with misgiving; it was only too obvious that they would not be rolling over any roads that day. The mechanics merely grunted when Darmono approached them. Japar now came forward with a noble proposition. He would walk to Leuwidamar, he said, and get our driver to come and fetch us. We agreed enthusiastically to his suggestion and as soon as he had gone we chose a shady spot under some trees and stretched on the grass. The sun was shining with a burning intensity on our side of the river but the territory we had just left looked grey and sullen. I glanced across at the tangled hills. How impenetrable and ferocious they appeared to be from here! How difficult to believe they are the abode of some of the gentlest people on this earth! We had not seen the snakes that Japar had promised us; we had not even been bitten by mosquitoes. And yet all the time we were in the jungle I had had the uneasy feeling that we were trespassing and being frowned upon by invisible observers—but this is characteristic of most jungles. I had experienced the same sensation in the Sumatra jungles three years before.

The rusty, rickety Ministry car came bouncing down the turfy track three hours later. We hailed it with joy and relief. The driver was in a gleeful mood too and we bounced all the way back to Leuwidamar over a track that only became a road when we approached a rubber estate. It was a jolting drive with a splendid view of the Baduis' hills behind us, but the car never forgave us for driving it so hard. It waited to take its revenge until nightfall when we were on a dark, deserted road three miles from the market town of Panggerang, then it suddenly turned feverish and began to send up plumes of smoke like an angry volcano. Our driver had no tools and all he could do was scratch his head and look puzzled while Darmono and I sat on the grassy banks at the side of the road where we were promptly attacked by mosquitoes. Soon a crowd of children gathered from out of the darkness. There was hardly any traffic on the road. Two private cars passed us hurriedly and refused to stop in answer to our signal of distress. Perhaps they were afraid we might be bandits. It is difficult to tell which is the most secure at night: the jungle with its prowling beasts or the dim country roads infested by human fanatics and outlaws. I wondered idly if I was being bitten by malaria mosquitoes. It was too dark to know. In the light it is always possible to distinguish them from the harmless variety, because malaria-carrying mosquitoes stand upon their heads to bite. I began to imagine a whole battalion of these tiny acrobats performing their nefarious antics upon my arms and legs but I tried to console myself with the reflection that I must have been fully immunized against infection by now thanks to my daily intake of paludrin tablets.

At last a lorry came trundling down the road. It not only stopped to find out what was the matter with us but its three occupants vied vociferously with each other in diagnosing the cause of our trouble. In the end they decided that the malady was grave but they patched us up and said we ought to be able to limp as far as Panggerang at a slow pace, but that they would drive behind us in case we had further trouble and had to be towed. From time to time our driver paused beside a rice-field from where he fetched a can full of water to placate the blistering engine.

When we eventually reached Panggerang, the helpful lorry-drivers left us to crawl up the drive leading to the local governor's palatial abode. I waited in the car while Darmono went in to inform the governor of our plight and ask for hospitality. (There are no hotels in these small out of the way towns where travellers are almost unknown.) He returned after a while to say that the governor and his wife had agreed to put us up but that they did not seem to be overjoyed at the prospect.

These imposing official residences, with lofty rooms and columned porticoes, are the same all over Java. They are all equally white, rigid, and aloof, a convincing symbol of administrative power. No doubt they were well run when they were occupied or supervised by the Dutch Residents for whom they were built, but the Javanese who have taken over since the Dutch left look ill at ease in them. They are not accustomed to so much space, they have not got enough money to furnish them as they should be, and they neglect the plumbing. As a result, the new Javanese officials and their families appear to be camping rather than living—in a vast, rapidly decaying mausoleum.

The governor of Panggerang spoke no English and he apologized for the lack of comfort, while his wife plied us with tea and coconut cakes and a knot of male guests stared at us pensively. They were still conscious of the difference in standards of living between whites and browns; moreover, they were evidently not used to being accepted as they are. I felt acutely embarrassed by their self-consciousness but I think they felt a little more at ease when I assured them through Darmono that a room to myself with a real bed in it was the very height of luxury after our recent experiences in the jungle.

Our hosts came from Central Java, where people still cling to an old-fashioned pattern of formal courtesy. It was only in the course of our late breakfast next morning that we learned why they had listened to Darmono's tale of our woes with ill-repressed consternation. Their eldest son was getting married at Bandung that day and they had arranged to leave Panggerang by car at dawn so as to arrive in good time for the ceremony. Our arrival had upset these plans for in their role of hosts they were bound by etiquette to minister to our needs and breakfast with us. Unwittingly we had delayed the wedding and upset their entire day. No wonder they had been dismayed to see us! 'If only you had told us last night,' I exclaimed, when this piece of information was at last imparted to us, 'there was no need for you to stay until we were awake!' But they only smiled. They went off at last after breakfast with a minimum of fluster but I am afraid that the memory of their son's wedding-day will for ever be marred by our inopportune visit!

PART III

JOURNEY TO A PALACE

I MEET THE SULTAN AND LEAVE FOR JOGJAKARTA

ONLY a few minutes after my return to Djakarta, the telephone rang and Soedjatmoko's soft voice came on the line. He had acted as go-between for me with the *kraton* (or palace) of Jogjakarta since I had written from London to ask how an introduction could be effected. 'The Sultan would like to meet you for lunch tomorrow to fix the date of your departure for Jogjakarta. Is that okay?'

I just had time to wash my hair, shake out the last particles of red jungle dust, and adjust myself to the transition from lowly Badui to high-born artistocrat before meeting his Royal Highness Hamengku Buwono IX. The active public existence of a Sultan in a new Republic like Indonesia seems at first sight to be rather anomalous. But Hamengku Buwono is different from the type of man usually associated with the title of Sultan. He is also very different from his father, who lived according to the old traditions and in grand Eastern style. Hamengku has moved with the times and it may disappoint romantic readers to learn that he actually *works*, wears a bush shirt on the job, drives his own car and often gives lifts to peasants and students whom he meets on his way. In some respects he leads a double life: a public life as head of the special area of Jogjakarta (which has a mainly peasant population of two million people) with offices in the centre of the city of Jogjakarta, and a private life in the *kraton* among his courtiers and vast family of Javanese aristocrats who pay homage to him in his role of hereditary ruler endowed with special, even supernatural, powers.

Hamengku Buwono gained enormous prestige during the revolutionary days before Indonesia won her independence. Affluent native rulers usually side with foreign occupiers, but the Sultan refused Dutch offers and helped the Nationalists. His palace kitchen was turned into guerrilla headquarters and it was in Jogjakarta—one of the two age-old cultural centres of Java—that the first independent Indonesian Government was formed under the presidency of 'Bung' (brother) Sukarno.

In recognition of his services, the Republicans have made the Sultan the administrative head of his province for life. Officially, the title of Sultan carries no powers except within the square mile of the palace grounds (Hamengku owns no land—his ancestors were shortsighted enough to part with all they owned to the Dutch). Unofficially, however, the Sultan's influence is considerable; he is revered by the people of his province and even outside its boundaries as a descendant of kings as well as for his affable personality.

Next day, Soedjatmoko came to fetch me in his car and he drove me to our rendezvous with the Sultan in the 'Java Restaurant' which—in spite of its name—is Chinese. Their crabs' legs in sour sauce are sought after by all gourmets, from the foreign correspondents in the capital to the Sultan of Jogjakarta whenever he comes into town.

'There he is,' said Soedjatmoko as we drove up to the open terrace, pointing to a solitary figure seated at one of the front tables. Nobody could have looked more democratic, yet at the same time no other man in shirtsleeves could have looked more obviously aristocratic. The Sultan rose to greet us with a friendly smile of recognition for Soedjatmoko and a slightly more reserved smile for me. He appeared to be shy, but this was probably due to Javanese restraint. He spoke softly in excellent English which he had learned in a Dutch school. So this was the Sultan of Jogjakarta, the descendant of the turbulent, hot-headed gentleman whom Sir Stamford Raffles had treated so severely a little over a hundred years ago! How times have changed since the despotic days of the nineteenth century. . . . This pleasant young Javanese ruler, dressed in the same short-sleeved white shirt as all the other men in the restaurant, courteously offering a cigarette and ordering iced tea for an English writer . . . could he really be the Sultan of Jogjakarta? It was enough to make his great-grandfather turn in his grave! But it was enough to make *me* feel spontaneously sympathetic towards him. So many of the new Indonesian middle class lack personality because they are still uncertain of themselves. What a pleasant change it was to meet a real, self-confident person. The peasants of the jungle and the aristocrats—the palace and the jungle—it is in these two ends of the social scale that one finds the most genuine people in Java. They are also the least Westernized, content to be themselves without aping some half-comprehended alien ideal.

The Sultan is in his early forties, but the Javanese—both men and women—have a way of looking much younger than their age. He is of medium height, light-skinned, with dark thoughtful eyes that suddenly light up behind his spectacles with a disarming, schoolboyish smile. He has a wide, generous mouth and rather large nostrils. When he smiles, he radiates such warmth, such genuine kindliness and tolerance that it is easy to understand why his people feel such affection for him. Later on in Jogjakarta I got to know him better in the course of long *tête-à-tête* conversations. Beneath his Western education, the Sultan is very Javanese and, to quote the expression used in the classic shadow plays or *wayang*: 'a man of refinement'—the Javanese equivalent of 'a gentleman'. (I should perhaps use the past tense, for this Javanese ideal is as moribund as the ideal of an English gentleman. A 'new movement' hero is in the making but he has not quite crystallized. Nor has the novelist, his biographer. Both will probably emerge within the next ten years.)

Over lunch we discussed the details of my stay in Jogjakarta and I explained at length all that I was anxious to find out while I was there. The Sultan nodded from time to time and Soedjatmoko occasionally intervened to exclaim: 'All this will take time!' to which the Sultan replied: 'That's perfectly all right—she can stay as long as she likes. My brother, Prince Prabuningrat, is expecting her . . . he will look after her.'

After lunch, the Sultan drove me back to the bungalow in his bright blue Chevrolet and two days later I set off for Jogjakarta to discover what goes on behind the high walls of the palace in this republican day and age.

*   *   *   *

If I had chosen to travel to Jogjakarta by aeroplane the journey would only have lasted a couple of hours instead of twelve, but I would have missed some superb tropical scenery. A railway journey in Java is full of exciting possibilities, as a Chinese friend pointed out before my departure. 'To begin with,' he warned me unemotionally, 'your train will arrive several hours late, but in addition it may be derailed or held up by bandits . . . anything can happen in this country!' Nothing so adventurous befell me, however. The only change in the normal run was that we were obliged to stop frequently to pick up peasant passengers at out-of-the-way stations, because several local trains had been cancelled owing to a fuel shortage. The peasant folk squeezed in barefoot, laden with babies and live fowls, especially cocks that crowed unceasingly in the cramped space of their bamboo baskets.

I left tumultuous Djakarta in style, splendidly alone in a lime-green, first-class, air-conditioned compartment. I generally prefer to travel third class when I am abroad so as to be able to talk to and observe as many different people as possible, but the exhausting heat of Djakarta had made me temporarily unsociable.

I reached my carriage in the wake of two ruffianly porters who charged the crowds like guffawing bulls and were reduced to helpless laughter when my suitcases slipped off their shoulders on to the platform. There was only one other passenger in the first-class Pullman—a railway official who was travelling free of charge. He mistook me for an American. When a white person turns out not to be Dutch there is only one alternative: he or she must be an American with pockets full of dollars. When you inform your interlocutors that you are *Inggris* (English) they usually look politely blank. The railway official tried his few words of English on me, but they were inadequate—like my own limited Indonesian vocabulary—to involve us in an absorbing conversation. I asked him at what time we were due to arrive at

Jogjakarta and he pulled out an impressive chart, ornamented with arrows pointing in various directions, which appeared to have been printed for the private use of railway employees. There were only two trains a day to Jogjakarta but the chart was so complex that it took him at least five minutes to decipher and even then he announced the arrival time of the train that had left two hours before ours. On occasions such as this one wonders how long it will take before the Javanese can run their country efficiently. At other times, however, one has pleasant surprises as on the day before I left Djakarta when I found a Javanese technician who repaired my complicated tape-recorder very ably. It is premature to pass judgments, but the constant ups and downs, particularly the more frequent downs, tend to strain taut European nerves.

A barefoot child with the wideawake eyes of those who have had to start fending for themselves at a very early age pushed a sheaf of gaudy coloured magazines under my nose. Some of them were Indonesian imitations of our popular Western magazines with their never-ending display of feminine charms, while others were genuinely American and quickly snapped up by the many Javanese admirers of the American way of life, including their films, that appear regularly upon Indonesian screens. I was about to write 'city screens' but that would be inaccurate, for I have seen posters displaying half-naked girls with highly developed bosoms, and brutish gangsters, even on small country hoardings. No wonder native views on our morals are not always wholly to our advantage.

They can't have enough of American films. Indonesian film directors with their long-winded stories find it hard to compete with so much 'action' and novelty. There are exceptions, of course. Indian films are popular too, and an Egyptian film on the life of the Prophet Mohammed was enjoying a tremendous box-office success at that moment. There were several fighting scenes in it, but the main one, depicting a Cromwellian orgy of idol-smashing by the Prophet's followers, was not considered 'impressive enough' by Indonesian fans of Hollywood productions.

For the first three hours of the journey the landscape was monotonously flat and swampy, but a transformation took place when we reached the sharp green spine of volcanoes that divide the insipid northern plains from the exuberant southern half of the island. This kind of landscape makes you sit up. It is a lustful landscape, impelling you to stretch out your arms towards it; the mountains have been shaped by a divinity with an obsession for cones and pyramids whose work was followed up by another with a passion for a dense camouflage of vegetation. The result of their joint efforts looks unreal, perhaps because it is unlike anything we have in Europe. The total effect is almost too stagey. We would never dream of questioning the logic of any particular arrangement of scenery in Britain, unless it was an artificial creation by Capability Brown. We accept what nature has bestowed on our land. Not so in Java, which has so obviously been fashioned by deities with individual and rather extravagant aesthetic ideas. 'Why did you do this? What were you thinking of when you did that?' one feels like asking the creators of these tropical riots. However did they discover such luminous greens, I wondered as I looked out from my compartment on to a gigantic canopy of interlaced arches, each one springing from a different tree and in a different shade from that of its neighbours. The darkest greens in the background were shot through with gleams of light that winked slowly like sleepy stars. Dappled bamboos clung close together like timid deer, pretending to be frail. Festoons of pale gold or lilac blossoms tossed upon high branches were triumphantly shaken by black-faced monkeys that bared their teeth as our train went by, like the laughing, apricot-coloured children who waved at us so gaily a hundred feet below.

Between the mountains and their furious growth stretched the unending, placid sheen of paddy-fields under water, separated by dark ridges of mud. This was the only earth visible. The rest had been transmuted into a vast mirror, broken into a thousand pieces, each one reflecting coconut palms at the fringes and clouds in the centre, clouds whose immensity and ever-changing convolutions are a constant source of enjoyment in this land.

The rice-fields were as restful to the eye as the volcanoes were disturbing; in some areas the young shoots were already nearly a foot above water and of a dazzling green; in others farther on, from which the water had been drained, the ripe stalks were protected from predatory birds by young human scarecrows reclining upon flimsy bamboo platforms who clapped their tiny hands and uttered shrill cries whenever any winged creature appeared on the horizon. Beyond them on the dusty roads men and women were carrying golden sheaves of rice, soft as human hair, to lay them in rows along the edge of a field or upon a low mud wall for a last toasting touch of the sun.

There was no dining-car on the train but an obsequious little attendant in white brought me the standard lunch provided by Indonesian Railways: a soup plate filled with fried rice and chillies, topped by a thin overfried egg and a few cubes of raw cucumber. This was followed by the inevitable banana and a glass of local coffee. Sages always advise us not to crave after food: they ask us to eat merely in order to live. There is no virtue in following this precept in Indonesia.

Soon after twilight, a pale Chinese lantern of a moon was suspended between the palms. At first, I mistook it for the cupola of Jogjakarta's mosque—the new mosque at the edge of the river, designed by a Dutch architect.

THE STONE BELLS OF THE BOROBODUR

TWENTY miles west of Jogjakarta, close to the toffee-coloured river Progo, against a backdrop of serrated hills, stands the Borobodur—the most impressive monument ever built in honour of the Buddha. Its origin is mysterious. There are no records to tell us who built the shrine or the name of the sovereign who ordered it to be set in this miniature Himalayan landscape.

According to the native chronicles of Java, the first colonists from India arrived about A.D. 75 led by a prince of Gujerat, but they did not settle permanently. In 603 a great fleet brought five thousand men, including agriculturists and craftsmen, who established a Gujerati dynasty in the centre of the island; but in 750, when the Borobodur was erected, a rival Indian dynasty, the Cailendras, were in power. Their rulers must therefore be regarded as the founders of the Borobodur. Although 90 per cent of the Javanese have been converted to Mohammedanism since the sixteenth century, many of them continue to believe that the Borobodur is a powerful spiritual stronghold. Peasants come to burn incense and leave rose petals every day at the grey feet of the rows of Dhyani-Buddhas who sit crosslegged with downcast eyes, enfolded in perpetual meditation.

There are no remains of any city round the Borobodur. It stands alone, off the road to Magelang, with only a flimsy bamboo village or two in its immediate vicinity and the little Chandi Mendut temple with its colossal figure of the seated Buddha flanked by disciples, guarding its approach.

The rice was swaying in the fields as we drove out of Jogjakarta towards the hills. Rows of slender, blue-clad figures protected by bamboo hats as wide as parasols were bending over the stems, noiseless but for the sharp whisper of a small bamboo knife held between the second and third fingers of their right hand. I smiled affectionately at a black tea kettle balanced precariously at the edge of one of these fields—an object beloved by the Javanese almost as much as by the British. Many, many are the interruptions for tea-drinking in Javanese rice-fields and it was pleasant to find this friendly, pot-bellied form so far away from home. Although this particular kettle was alone, it did not look at all abandoned or lost and was waiting for the return of its owner with the self-composure peculiar to its species.

The country road was streaked with toylike people on their way to market—toylike not so much because of their small stature, but because of their jerky gait that made them look as if they had been wound up by clockwork. They walked so fast that I was constantly expecting them to wind down and come to a sudden standstill.

Clouds were beginning to tip over the hills with that wavelike effect so often reproduced by Chinese painters. It is rare to find the background to the Borobodur completely uncovered. The hills try to make up for their lack of Himalayan snow by mantles of cloud and mist. It is even rarer to be able to distinguish the smoking pyramid of Mount Merapi from the summit of the Borobodur but when one does it is a splendid sight.

At last the grey mass of the shrine appeared, unspectacular from a distance owing to its reduced dimensions and the darkness of the volcanic stone, but more and more intriguing as one draws closer and the details of its construction and silhouette are revealed. This astonishing silhouette with its myriad pinnacles like mountain peaks surmounting inverted lotus flowers (that to us look more like bells) is—to quote Havell: 'A poet's dream of India's heavenly city Himalaya, the Abode of Snow.' It was to Mount Kailasa in the Himalayas that the Buddha is alleged to have gone when he was deified, and the Himalayas represent the shrine of all the gods. On Mount Kailasa the Divine Thinker sits in his icy cell controlling the universe by the power of Yoga. There is to be found the heavenly staircase by which the Buddha and many of the Avatars descended to be born on earth. There is the source of the four world rivers which water the four great continents, or the four petals of the World Lotus.

It was dusk by the time we arrived and the lime-coloured moon was beginning its slow awesomely silent ascent behind the stone bells, throwing their pinnacles into sharp relief. The air is fresh up here. The difference in temperature between the hills and the plains of Java is quite remarkable. (The Ministry of Information official who had accompanied me on this to him incomprehensible jaunt found it unbearably cold and he took cover in the café built about fifty yards away from the shrine on a little green plateau; he was relieved when I told him that I would prefer to wander round by myself.)

Incandescent cigars—fireflies' tapering bodies—gave me sufficient light to find my way up the steep stone steps that lead to the spiralling galleries. The pilgrim who climbs the hill upon which the Borobodur is built and the long flights of steps mounting to the stone bells which crown the summit, inevitably thinks of the great northern pilgrimages of India. Beneath is a wide, fertile plain, like the valley of the Ganges at the foot of the Himalayas. In the distance are majestic mountain tops—not covered with snow but reminiscent of nature's destructive moods, for all of them are volcanoes, extinct or alive.

Those who follow the wide processional path up to the topmost pinnacle perform, symbolically, the same rite as the Buddhist when he first visits the sacred places associated with the various lives of the Great Teacher on earth, and then climbs the heights of Kailasa to bow down in worship, as if in the presence of the Lord Buddha.

From the lowest gallery of the Borobodur one begins to pass in review the previous lives of the Buddha as told in the legends of the *Gatakamala* or 'Wreath of Flowers'. Here for instance is a splendid stone galleon veering off its course, illustrating the tale of the Buddha's life as a steersman in the port of Suparaga, where merchants longing for a prosperous voyage once asked him to embark with them. He went out of compassion in spite of his great age and infirmities. What a voyage it was . . . an aquatic inferno, through the Abode of the Snakes—the Great Ocean haunted by weird fishes 'wearing silver armour, with fierce looks and ugly noses that resembled a quadruped's hoof'—the sea of fire-garlands—the topaz-coloured waves of the Kusamalin Sea, and the dreadful Mare-Mouth where the submarine fire resides. But thanks to the Great Being's power and love of truth the current of the wind changed and caused the vessel to return safely to port, miraculously loaded with beryls and sapphires.

The sculptured panels wind round and round, covering an aggregate length of three miles. One of the loveliest scenes among many which it is not within the scope of this book to describe, shows the Prince Siddhartha who, having at last attained Nirvana (the ending of earthly desires) bathes in the river Nairanyana. Here, his trials and temptations over, he is the Buddha—the noble, purified soul. The heavenly bliss within him affects every creature that comes near. The spirits of the upper air shower scented flowers upon the river; the water sprites raise their heads to pay him homage. On the opposite side of the river three pilgrims in the dress of Javanese princes bow down before him. Most charming of all is the doe who whispers the joyful tidings to her little one, which turns its head wonderingly to look upon Him whom all nature worships.

When one reaches the higher terraces, the sculptured panels are replaced by the great stone bells through which the forms of the Dhyani-Buddhas are only dimly visible. (A Dhyani-Buddha is a Buddha supposed to exist as a kind of spiritual essence in the higher regions of abstract thought.) They represent the regions of formlessness, the gradations of mystic meditation and their corresponding worlds.

Finally, at the very summit, the pilgrim reaches the symbolic Kailasa or centre of the cosmos, where Gautama Buddha sat calling the earth to witness his enlightenment as he had done under the bodhi tree at Gaya, invisible except to the adept in Yoga. Here at Borobodur the image was entirely embedded in the masonry of the cupola which crowns the shrine, where no human eyes could see it. In this way the builders symbolized the highest insight, the supreme goal of the devout Buddhist.

A great black-and-white bird brushed past me as I sat upon the highest terrace and listened to distant *penchak* drums throbbing between the coconut palms. Bats began to weave in and out of the bells. A cool breeze stirred the palm fronds down below and caused the fireflies to twinkle unsteadily as they scaled the heights. Nature is very close to the Borobodur, which is as it should be, for the Buddha loved all the creatures of the forests. We read that 'as a young prince in his palace before he set out in search of Truth, a dove seized by a hawk, a dog dying from snakebite, filled him with horror. The roarings of wild beasts in the show-men's cages seemed to him even more dreadful, more sorrowful, than the cries of their victims and caused him to tremble with compassion.' We are also told that during his meditations in the cold winter nights when he had abandoned his luxurious home, a gazelle, attracted by his gentleness, licked the Buddha's icy feet. He touched her and finding that she was frozen, took her in his arms to warm her against his heart.

★   ★   ★   ★

Eventually I stumbled down to the plateau and walked across to the café where I was gleefully hailed by Leah who informed me that she had been buying fruit in the village for her vegetarian supper. She had already settled in, she said, and she looked as if she was enjoying herself, until she tried smoking a *kretek*—or clove-scented Javanese cigarette. 'They are putting up a bed for me in the toilet,' she announced triumphantly. 'I'm going to have a wonderful night. What air! It sure is good to breathe again after all that heat in the town.' I was not quite so sanguine, however. 'There's room for you in the car if you want to change your mind,' I said, but she refused.

Next day at noon I met a subdued Leah hobbling up the hotel drive in Jogjakarta. 'I *thought* you were rather quiet when I said I was going to have a good night,' she glumly remarked when she saw me. 'That's because I didn't want to be hypocritical,' I replied. 'How was it then?' Leah gave a short, sarcastic laugh. 'About the worst night I have ever spent in my life. Do you know there was no mattress to sleep on, only a board and a bamboo mat? That's what these people call a bed. Then one of the women insisted upon sleeping in the same room, on the floor; she kept an oil lamp on all through the night and the window firmly shut because of mosquitoes. They didn't have a *klambu*. Am I feeling sore all over this morning! And as for that moon I went up for—it disappeared behind a cloud almost as soon as you left.' 'Anyway,' I remarked brightly, 'there weren't any bandits up there, were there? My driver was scared stiff of them all the way back to Jogjakarta.' Now that you mention it,' said Leah, 'I *did* hear a few shots being fired through the night, but I guessed it was a peasant shooting rabbits or something. Bandits . . . well now, I never thought of *that*! How very exciting!' She left for Bali that afternoon. Two days later I received a postcard from her scrawled: 'Wonderful temples, splendid dancers', and two months after a postcard from Japan inscribed: 'Land of Art and Sensitivity!' Since then I have heard nothing more. I still feel a slight twinge of conscience about that moon over the Borobodur and Leah's bad night because of it, in the converted toilet. I should have insisted and brought her back in the Ministry car. However, I console myself with the reflection that uncomfortable experiences are what friends like to hear about most when one returns from far-away places. People are invariably delighted to hear that we fortunate travellers did not enjoy ourselves *all* the time!

I AM RECEIVED AT THE *KRATON*

TWO days after my arrival in Jogjakarta the Information Service car called to take me to the *kraton* for my first meeting with the Sultan's eldest brother, Prince Prabuningrat.

We drove down Malioboro and into a wide square called the *alun-alun*, through a pagoda-shaped gateway typical of *kraton* architecture. The principal approach to a Javanese palace is always from the north; the sides of the *alun-alun* are adorned by rows of banyan trees on whose branches hang cages of that highly-prized Javanese songster the *perkutut* which looks like a dove with a pale blue head and rosy breast. These *perkututs* belong to the owners of the stalls that have encroached upon the *alun-alun* in these irreverent modern times. In the old days tournaments, processions, and military exercises were held here and the Sultan was in the habit of showing himself to his subjects once a week with much ceremony; it was, in fact, the Javanese Field of Mars.

Two immense banyan trees occupy the centre of the square. They are much thought of and many citizens are to be seen walking round them in procession every Thursday evening. Various ceremonies of a religious character take place on Thursday evenings throughout Java—that is, on the eve of the Muslim day of rest—and a special place is allotted to them in the Javanese calendar which—incidentally—counts weeks from one 'market day' to the next. The people still believe in calendar lore, according to which certain days are more auspicious than others; it is also considered unlucky to travel in a specific direction on special days. Since petty thieves nearly always follow these directions implicitly, the Javanese police are never without one of these calendars in their pockets.

Sir Stamford Raffles would not recognize the *kraton* nowadays.

It has become democratized, especially in the ten years since the revolution, yet in many ways it is still an astonishing combination of ancient and modern. The contrast is visible from the *alun-alun* which is now practically a public fairground. At one end of it (mercifully half-concealed by dignified banyans) a garish cinema displays the same type of bosomy posters that we see in Piccadilly Circus, while at the opposite end is a pavilion in which the traditional arts and crafts of Java are taught to the young by *kraton* instructors. On holidays, the centre of the *alun-alun* is studded with booths full of balloons and jolly bamboo toys: Garuda birds, tigers, elephants, spotted snakes, miniature sunshades made from the pages of used copybooks which have been painted and pleated out of recognition until one looks closely and sees the childish scrawls beneath. For a few cents, you can buy an awesome green-and-blue dragon, or a mask of some well-known shadow-play puppet.

After passing through the gateway at the end of the *alun-alun* we came to the actual entrance of the palace, called the *pagalaran* or 'place spread with mats'. This is a double pavilion, which was used as a waiting-room for courtiers before they were ushered into the Sultan's presence. A spacious flight of steps leads from this to a terraced pavilion, the *sitinggil* which means, literally, 'the high place' or terrace upon which the Sultan gave audience on public occasions and where certain important ceremonies were performed. Here I have to use the past tense because the present Sultan has placed the pavilions of the *pagalaran* at the disposal of the university students, who are short of lecture halls. The palace entrance is constantly choked with a stream of eager young boys and girls who park their gleaming bicycles in the precincts of the picturesque palace guards. These dignified descendants of the old ceremonious days glide barefoot in sombre sarongs among the noisy modern generation in Western clothes—as anachronistic in their quiet Javanese way as the Tudor Beefeaters at the Tower of London.

Most of the Venetian chandeliers in the pavilion for medical students had recently been smashed in a student affray between the 'puritanical' and the 'tolerant' factions of Muslim youth, all because of the visiting Austrian football team. The Sultan is an ardent football fan and the President of Jogjakarta's Football Association. The local team is so good that it had just beaten the Austrians—to their surprise—by 3–0. The most Westernized and broadminded among the university students thought that it would have been a friendly gesture to organize a dance for the Austrians in the palace pavilion. This plan, however, was violently opposed by those orthodox Mohammedan students who disapprove both of jazz and the close proximity of the sexes in Western-style dancing. As a result of their discussion —during which more than words were involved—the Sultan lost his Venetian glass chandeliers! The youth, and even the adults of Jogjakarta, are far sterner than those of Solo, only forty miles away—and the residence of the *Susuhunan* who used to style himself the 'Emperor of Java'. The present young *Susuhunan* is far from being of the same calibre as the Sultan of Jogjakarta. 'The best lovers come from Solo,' I was informed by some; 'Solo is full of bad women,' I was told by others—depending upon their point of view.

These two territories of Jogjakarta and Solo used to be united under the *Susuhunan*, but towards the beginning of the eighteenth century there was a rebellion by one branch of the family. The Dutch Government, practising the old imperial technique of 'divide to conquer' played its part too, with the result that in 1755 the rebel faction had settled down in quasi-independence at Jogjakarta under a separate ruler, with the title of Sultan of Mataram.

Beyond the *sitinggil* a variety of walled enclosures and gates lead to the different dwellings of the Sultan, his large family, and his personnel. The external walls of the *kraton* are imitations of European fortifications with bastions, parapets, moats, and glacis; the whole forms a walled town about three miles in circumference with a population of twenty thousand inhabitants. The Sultan, as I mentioned before, owns no land and in addition he lost a good deal of money during the Japanese occupation of Java, so that he must find it extremely difficult to make ends meet. In his role of head of the special province of Jogjakarta he is paid a salary by the Government of Indonesia, but I doubt whether this is adequate to cover his large palace expenses. Fortunately, it is considered to be such an honour to work in the *kraton* that his large household staff serve him for next to nothing. Economy, however, is being practised as never before; ceremonies are being curtailed, both for diplomatic as well as financial reasons, because there are envious Republicans in Jogjakarta who would probably like to see the *kraton* and its aristocracy swept away with the dust of ages. If they succeed—and I pray that they will not, for the people love their Sultan—the best of Java's heritage will go with them; the *kraton* is more than a palace, more than a Court imbued with old-fashioned ideals of courtesy and etiquette—it is a cultural depository of incalculable value. Java does not possess so rich a heritage that she can afford to cast even a particle of it away. One of the Sultan's Javanese titles means 'axis, or pivot of the world'. This is, of course, an exaggeration, but I am convinced that the *kraton* and the traditional values it represents are the spiritual pivot of Java.

★   ★   ★   ★

To reach Prince Prabuningrat's office we drove round the *alun-alun*, turned left into a street full of ambling *betjaks*, then right under a gateway built by the same Portuguese architect who designed the now ruined Water Palace beyond the *kraton*. He evolved a tropical Baroque style which probably looks more attractive in its present state of semi-decay than it did when it was new; peeling stucco reveals the volcanic stone beneath and the grey and white scrolls against the background of coconut palms are haunted by a decadent, extravagant charm. This gateway leads into the street where the best silversmiths of Jogjakarta hammer away at their lovely craft; another right turn takes us down a narrow road of bungalows and shacks; a tame monkey stretched wantonly on the ground is having his fleas picked off him by two earnest children; a *betjak* boy, obviously off duty, squats outside his home with two of his cronies to gossip over a scented *kretek* cigarette. The little gardens are thick with palms and bamboo trees; *perkutut* cages line the eaves of the houses. Strangely enough, this countrified scene is on the *kraton's* very doorstep and the road ends abruptly before a gateway leading into yet another of the *kraton's* many courtyards.

We stop at last in front of a new building that looks like a private dwelling. In the porch a group of people are sitting round a table while a spectacled gentleman, obviously a person of some authority, sits in the centre writing cursively upon an enormous ledger; more people, men and women, sit on benches, waiting for their turn. Before I have time to ask what this is all about we are ushered into an office at the back where an unusually tall Javanese gentleman rises from behind his desk and advances to greet me with a welcoming smile. I shake hands at last with Prince Prabuningrat and begin my initiation into Javanese Court life.

There is little resemblance between the Sultan and the Prince—it is true that they had different mothers—but both have one feature in common: a warm, open smile. Unlike the Sultan, Prince Prabuningrat dresses in the traditional *kraton* style: a brown and cream sarong, sandals, a flat turban knotted at the back of the head, and the high-necked shirt with tightly-buttoned sleeves worn by every male member of the palace household. The Prince was educated in a Dutch university after having been sent out of the *kraton* at a very early age. With his brother the Sultan he lived with a Dutch teacher and his family—first in Jogjakarta and later at Magelang—returning to the *kraton* during his vacations (a similar system was in vogue with the English aristocracy of the seventeenth century). Perhaps their father, Hamengku Buwono VIII, wished his sons to be able to understand the Dutch mentality so that they would know how to deal and parry with them later on in life; this attitude caused some resentment among the early Indonesian Nationalists, who feared that the princes would become 'too Westernized' and removed from their people. Their fears, however, have proved to be completely without foundation. There is no more sincere patriot in the whole of the archipelago than His Royal Highness and his family. In the same way, most of the Indians and Asians who come to study in Great Britain return home without any fundamental change of heart towards their native land. Soon after they begin to share the lives of their own people again, they shed their thin, recently-acquired Western veneer. They are bound to compromise. It is amazing to see how quickly they revert to their ancestral habits and conform to their pattern of society. Family ties and influences count more in the East than in the West, and none can dissolve Western ways and notions more rapidly than a stern array of Eastern uncles and aunts (not to mention nearer relatives). Most Eastern boys are careful not to incur paternal and avuncular displeasure; they are also naturally easy-going and unconsciously inclined to ancestor-worship.

Nowhere in Java is the pattern of society and the rules laid down for the conduct of 'a man of refinement' more rigid than in the *kraton*, whose members, descended from the dynasties of the Hindu period, move with the poise and grace of an ageless aristocracy. And so it was not really so difficult for the Sultan and his brother, when they returned from Leyden in 1939, to merge into the enchanting setting of *srimpi* dances, gamelan music, and ceremonial which I had travelled so far to see. Some Western hobbies, however, have penetrated into the *kraton*; for instance, both the Sultan and the Prince are first-rate photographers and do all their own developing and enlarging. One of the first things I noticed in the Prince's office was part of his fine collection of portraits and landscapes; the next object to attract my attention was a picture of Rodin's *Hand of God*. The Prince has been approached by the Academy of Art to lecture on the history of art but although this is one of his favourite subjects he says that he 'does not possess the vocational urge of a professor'. His daily task at the *kraton*, which cannot be very congenial, is concerned with palace supplies—a formidable duty in view of the number of people within its walls. When he told me that he was also on the Executive Committee that deals with the administration of the new city mosque, I feared for a moment that he might be fanatical but I soon discovered that the Prince is typically 'Central Javanese', a people upon whom providence has bestowed that rarest of gifts—tolerance. Besides, it must be remembered that Islam penetrated into Indonesia from India and so reached them in a mystic, Hinduized form.

Fortunately for me, the Prince spoke English fluently, although he rarely has the opportunity of using it. He has a delectable sense of humour (this too is a Javanese trait) and he is extremely frank (this is *not* a common Javanese characteristic). I could not have had a more cultured and agreeable mentor during the many visits that followed this first glimpse of the labyrinthine *kraton*.

ROYAL GONGS AND COURT DANCERS

FROM the back of Prince Prabuningrat's office, where male clerks in turbans and sarongs sit incongruously behind large modern typewriters, we stepped into the courtyard where the most sumptuous royal sets of gamelan instruments are displayed. The gongs gleam in red, blue, and gold carved frames, casting long shadows on the polished floors of the two pavilions which shelter them from the scorching sun and the devastating rains. These gongs are the more majestic for being silent the year round with the exception of one special feast day. The great metal discs of varying sizes, with their raised nipples, now so still, are capable of rendering the sweetest sounds imaginable. They were fashioned by anonymous masters, contemporaries of the craftsmen who forged Javanese swords, or krisses, breathing magic powers into their exquisite handiwork. Both of these arts in which the occult—as always in Java—played an important role either for good or for evil, have disappeared with changing conditions. Krisses are no longer used except as sacred relics for ceremonial purposes; the gamelan is still played and taught in the *kraton* schools of music, but it is unlikely that magnificent royal sets will ever be ordered again.

A few years ago, a member of the Vienna opera heard one of the *kraton* gongs and was so impressed by its sonorous quality and other-world tone that he searched the whole of Java for a similar one to take back with him to Vienna, to be played in a special performance of *Parsifal*. Sir Stamford Raffles was equally intrigued by them and he had a complete gamelan set packed on board the S.S. *Fame*, which was to have carried him, his wife, and one hundred and twenty-three cases containing unique collections of Malay flora, fauna, and manuscripts back to England. Unfortunately, a fire broke out and destroyed the lot—to the everlasting sorrow of all historians and students of Malay and Indonesian lore.

But I wished to see and hear live instruments and musicians, so the Prince conducted me through a large white gateway guarded by two fat-bellied statues of *Rakshashas*—gargantuan giants from Hindu mythology not unlike our Gog and Magog—and two lean palace guards limply holding lances. They seem to be waiting —eternally—for a tournament or tiger fight, but these feudal pastimes were abandoned a hundred years ago. Raffles has left a graphic account of these fearful and once popular contests between reluctant jungle beasts:

'A large cage of bamboo is erected in the square and a tiger is admitted after having let a buffalo in first. The buffalo is stimulated by constant applications of boiling water, which is poured over him from the upper part of the cage, and of nettles which are fastened to the end of a stick and applied by persons seated in the same quarter. The tiger sometimes springs upon the buffalo at once. He generally however avoids the combat until goaded by sticks and roused by the application of burning straw when he starts to move round the cage and, upon being gored by the buffalo, seizes him by the neck, head or leg. The buffalo is often dreadfully torn and seldom survives the combat many days. In these entertainments, the Javans are accustomed to compare the buffalo to the Javan and the tiger to the European, and it may be readily imagined with what eagerness they look to the success of the former. The combat generally lasts from twenty minutes to half an hour when, if neither of them are destroyed, the animals are changed.'

The only present-day survivals of animal jousts are the officially forbidden cock-fights beloved of villagers (especially in East Java) and bull-fights; these are mild affairs compared to those of Spain, because no humans are involved and the bulls, unlike the bloodthirsty cocks, never fight to the death. Stakes are high; the vice here is gambling rather than blood-lust. Opium smoking, cockfighting, and gambling were the three major threats to public morals sternly forbidden by Raffles in the adjacent island of Sumatra, as well as by the puritanical Muslim sect of Patries. They were jungle-dwellers, which helps to confirm my theory about the moral purity of Indonesian jungles. There is none of the lasciviousness of Africa about them. This does not mean, however, that the men are disinterested in women. I have already referred to frivolous Solo, and there is a great deal of prostitution in other cities, notably in Djakarta, where the worship of Venus is not generally considered to be a vice. Women are still regarded as fecund dolls by the Javanese aristocracy, but outside this circle they are remarkably emancipated, highly intelligent, and as ruthless as the rest of womankind, under the deceptive camouflage of sarongs, demure buns at the nape of swanlike necks, and frail, hermaphrodite figures.

Behind the fierce, moustached *Rakshashas* lie the Sultan's offices and private apartments, built in pseudo-Moorish style, but with the addition of Venetian chandeliers and a row of Victorian plant-stands, blue and white like Delft ware, that belonged to the late Sultan. The carved wooden columns of the present Sultan's private apartments are decorated with a typically Javanese motif which recurs in every pavilion of the *kraton*: this is a sinuous line folding into a triple question mark. It is a 'protective' ornament and it reminded me vaguely of the three concentric circles of the Celts, whose language by the way is almost as rich in mystic content as old Javanese.

Scented frangipani trees fill this courtyard and shady reception pavilions with columns painted in green, red, and gold. Caged peacocks strut in a private menagerie to the right and wild birds warble full-throated songs from the blossom-laden branches above them, exulting in their freedom. They are ignored by the human beings around them who never attempt to watch their habits or imitate their cries. On the contrary, the Javanese have evolved a peculiar incantatory mode of singing, in which every note is made to strike the upper palate as if it were a particularly piercing gong. It is a style of singing adapted to incense-burning and sacrifices; divorced from ceremonial it sounds dehumanized to

Western ears. The singers were probably never intended to sound human but to represent disembodied wraiths from the spirit-world.

Every gamelan orchestra has three or four female vocalists. Those attached to Solo's *kraton* are said to spend a good deal of their leisure in princely bedrooms; not, however, the quavering little ladies of Jogjakarta, whose Sultan is usually too busy inspecting sugar-cane factories to be able to devote much time to more than his quadruple marital relationships.

The *kraton* musicians and vocalists practise every Thursday morning in the music pavilion of the courtyard where the royal *wayang* puppets are kept. There is only room for one pavilion here, instead of the usual two or three. The gamelan occupies one side of it and the *wayang* puppets rest face downwards in flat boxes between peacock feathers upon the other side.

The *kraton* players were squatting beside their instruments taking Javanese 'elevenses' when the Prince and I arrived upon the scene. Dainty white cups filled with honey-coloured tea were set between their bony thighs tightly wound in dark-blue sarongs, and empty cups sat beside the row of heelless black sandals waiting for their masters upon the pavilion steps. I placed my shoes beside them and the Prince slipped out of his sandals; then we padded barefoot over the cool marble floor and squatted in front of the gamelan to talk with the leader, a round-faced, jovial man bubbling over with good spirits and musical enthusiasm. His musicians, however, were a very different kettle of fish. All of them were hungry-looking in their leanness, solemn and sallow. This appears to be an occupational type of physique. I have never seen gamelan players look any different anywhere else. An earnest, bearded young American squatted beside the leader, taking copious notes which he generously passed over to me. Alas, I am not a musicologist, and his references to 'blown fifths' were wasted on me, except that they served to conjure up all manner of fantastic, dreamlike forms. I pictured a radiant set of golden figures of five, large as trumpets—elongated Swiss mountain trumpets—flat to start with and then swelling up ultimately to break like bubbles, ever so silently, above the tinkling metallophones.

I passed the notebook of 'blown fifths' back, together with a confession of ignorance which did not seem to surprise or dismay the young American in the least. He told me that he had been living in Jogjakarta for a year (in a kampong, to save money) and that his greatest ambition in life was to learn how to play every instrument in the gamelan; but since the ears of Western audiences are not on the whole pleasantly tickled by the titillations of a gamelan, I do not know how this young man is ever going to make a living out of his unusual knowledge. Maybe he will go on lecture tours in the United States and become famous as: 'The Only American Who Plays the Gamelan.' Or maybe he will end by going completely native and remain in Java for ever. He appeared to be popular with the Javanese. No doubt, being reincarnationists, they think that he must have been a gamelan player in a former existence.

The orchestra began to play an ancient, haunting tune composed for the annual 'knee-kissing ceremony' when the Sultan's male relatives assemble in the adjoining courtyard to pay him homage. Javanese music has been compared to 'moonlight and running water'—an apt description of its cold, relentless purity. To be able to understand and like it fully, one must be very close to elf-land, for it is a floating, tremulous, fairylike music. The rhythms flow in a pattern as complex as *penchak* movements, without a break. It is soft and peculiarly appropriate to people who walk barefoot and speak gently. Beside the gamelan, most of our Western orchestrated music sounds like a declaration of war. The gongs and drums of African peoples that serve to drive away evil spirits sound furious and aggressive, but Javanese gongs, combined with their liquid metallophones, and the plaintive Arabian violin or rebab, are more in the nature of an invocation to the gods, the humanized gods of the *wayang*; it is a music of phantom-ecstasy.

At times, the gamelan dwindles until it is no louder than grass-hoppers' wings in a summer meadow. This 'insect music' is at times almost too tenuous for human ears. As you listen, time flows pleasantly over and around you, while the vibrations eddy through your pores until you become one with the sound and, as in a mystic trance, lose your personal identity. I am convinced that like the Indian tune Maya Maha Gaula Raga, the gamelan is capable of stimulating the growth of flowers.

* * * *

At midday the court dancers glided into position to rehearse the dances of the classical repertoire—especially the *Srimpi*, or dance of the court ladies—that have been nurtured as carefully as hothouse plants in the *kratons* of Java. Perfected by countless generations of artists since the Hindu courts of the early Middle Ages, the palace dancers of Java are the epitome of sinuous sophistication. Here too, as in the gamelan, the movements flow, merging into each other like the gradual unfolding of water lilies, with a slight, highly-controlled aquatic swaying of the stem-like body. As with every difficult art, it looks easy, because of its unceasing, undulating smoothness. Once you have seen a *Srimpi* performance in the *kraton*, you are spoiled for life, for only here (and in the *kraton* of Solo) is this ritualistic dance preserved with an almost religious tenderness and attention to detail unmatched outside the palace walls. The royal *Srimpi* is performed by four girl dancers (in former times the Sultan's concubines, nowadays, his relatives) wearing crimson velvet, golden-fringed *kebayas*, and a golden headdress with a white plume in the centre. They are accompanied by four female attendants who carry the shields, bows and arrows used in the course of the surprisingly military portion of the dance. (Incidentally, the present Sultan's youngest wife is an accomplished *Srimpi* dancer.)

There is no more impressive spectacle than the slow, measured advance of the four plumed ladies who approach the pavilion with modestly lowered eyes and bare feet step by step, at the pace of imperial mourners, their reed-like figures straight but never rigid. On this occasion, the gamelan gongs are played loudly. One would like to be able to applaud this magnificent entry, but

Javanese etiquette forbids such vulgarity. All their emotion is inward.

Once the dancers reach the centre of the pavilion, they sit cross-legged in their brown and cream sarongs, hand-painted with the wavy *rusak* motif that used to be reserved for the members of the Court. The *rusak* is said to be a stylized, highly conventional representation of deer's antlers. How curious it is, this world-wide association of deer's antlers with ritual dances, from those worn by the prehistoric Dancing Sorcerer painted in a Pyrenean cave to the Pueblo Indians of New Mexico, not forgetting our own Abbots Bromley dancers.

A complete *Srimpi* performance lasts for three-quarters of an hour and is composed of many movements, each of which, as in Western ballet, is designated by a special technical term. When the dancers rise from the floor, after joining their little hands in front of their forehead and bowing in the Hindu form of saluta-tion known as the *sembah*, the hieratic tableau slowly comes to life; they rise at the tempo of a slow-motion picture with their knees bent, and revolve with their feet at right angles; now follows a swing sideways and a quick 'flying' movement on tiptoe, followed by the intricate *gedrok* or 'make-up' miming with eyes, arms, and hands. After the jerky 'bird movement' the flexible hands are bent backwards and forwards, covered by the stole (a similar gesture is found in Chinese dances, in which the wide sleeve is used instead of the stole).

After a sliding movement with the soles of the feet, called *kanser*, the shields and daggers are presented to the dancers by their attendants, then the bows and arrows. When this Amazonian display is over, they become demure again and trip lightly round the pavilion, raising one foot after the other very rapidly, for they are supposed to be walking upon unbearably hot, sun-drenched earth. The dance ends in the same sitting position as at the beginning, with the *sembah*, followed by a slow march out of the pavilion and back to the shelter of their carefully guarded, scented apartments.

The *Srimpi* is also performed by the *kraton's* male dancers by way of exercise and they in turn instruct others who teach it to pupils outside the palace. It is only during the last twenty years, however, that the *Srimpi* has been thus democratized. Before this time it was never danced by any other than the palace ladies and was considered to be in the nature of a sacred heirloom.

Another group, of nine dancers, called *bedoyos*, who wear their hair piled up in a bun at the top of their head in Javanese bridal fashion, are recruited from among the most comely young members of the *kraton*'s aristocracy and their duties include serving the Sultan at table, a task which they perform jointly with his wives.

The full classical repertoire includes a variety of dances, from warrior dances performed by 'officers' in blue and silver helmets, accompanied by ankle-bells, to the erotic *golak*, a complex solo dance which is said to stimulate sexual desire. (Even this, however, is eminently refined and very far removed from the vulgar belly-dancers of Egypt and Arabia.) Javanese men discuss women 'very much', I was told, but—unlike the Arabs and the English—they do not indulge in dirty stories. A Tunisian friend, whom I often relied upon for answers to questions which I dared not put to my bashful Javanese male acquaintances, imparted this piece of information to me with a note of surprised respect. But one must beware of tales told, or not told, to foreigners. To quote one instance: that awkward, strait-laced little man, John Crawfurd, who was the English Resident in Jogjakarta in Raffles's time, writes gravely in his account of Java that 'gross and abusive language never occurs in the people's intercourse. The harshest words which a Javanese will use towards an inferior are "goat" or "buffalo".' When I read this to the Prince, he burst out laughing and assured me that the Javanese language, which is rich in most expressions, is equally rich in unprintable swear words.

Most of Jogjakarta's rulers have taken a personal interest in dancing; they have even invented new dances to add to the palace repertoire; the present Sultan is no exception. He has devised a new ballet based on a Javanese wedding scene; the detailed steps of this dance were worked out by the *kraton* choreographers.

Incidentally, both the Sultan and the Prince used to shine as ball-room dancers during their student days in Europe but as soon as they became men and took up *kraton* life they regretfully put away these Western pastimes of their gay youth.

In the dancing schools outside the *kraton*, brand new and boring functional dances are being worked out by teachers with Leftish leanings; they had even introduced a workers' sit-down strike into one of their latest! A strike is never a thing of beauty, even when idealized by choreography. This novelty was proudly shown to the Chinese guests, but even they were a little taken aback by this *avant-garde* demonstration which they applauded with ill-feigned enthusiasm.

PALACE PUPPETS

THE next day was a Friday, and I returned to the *kraton* to watch the palace puppets being taken out of their boxes for their weekly airing. This task is entrusted to the *kraton* staff dedicated to the care of these curious, semi-venerated creatures; indeed, I am not sure what else I could call them, for they are more than lifeless puppets. Most of them represent humanized gods from the Hindu epics or heroes from Javanese history. So many entangled tales and wonderful exploits are attached to these shadowy, ghost-like figures that to dismiss them as puppets would be disrespectful.

The members of the royal household who, in the performance of their duties, touch personal objects belonging to the Sultan, wear a narrow brocade stole round their neck during the entire operation. When we approached the puppet pavilion I noticed that every one of the four servants squatting beside the royal banana trunk was wearing this badge of office and of honour which added to the ceremoniousness of the occasion. One of the four hastily rose to fetch two stiff, gilded chairs for me and the Prince, for it is well known that Europeans do not generally like to rest their posteriors upon the floor (they are also known to be clumsy about folding their long legs), but we waved the chairs away. The four men in blue sarongs exchanged friendly smiles with the Prince and bowed to me with the surprised pleasure of those who are not accustomed to seeing white people doing as the Javanese do when they are in Java. Apart from considerations of courtesy, I would have felt ludicrous sitting like an invalid in a bath-chair while the rest of the company squatted at my feet.

By the time we arrived the puppets were already out of their boxes and standing in the place allotted to them by tradition, to the right and left of the shadow screen. Their status extended from menial characters one foot high to royal personages and scowling giants rising to three and four feet, including the convolutions of their splendid headdress and the tight black curls of their rolled-up buns. They are cut out of buffalo hide, tastefully coloured and gilded because although only their shadows appear on the screen in front of which the women and children are seated, their full glory is revealed to the privileged menfolk sitting on the other side where the *dalang* or Master of Ceremonies manipulates them, surrounded by the musicians of the puppet's gamelan.

As I wished to photograph a couple of the handsomest puppets in the collection, I asked one of the *kraton dalangs* if he would kindly carry a pair out to the sunlight, the interior of the pavilion being in deep shade. Unwittingly, however, I had selected two characters who never appear together in *wayang* stories and I was informed that it would be quite out of the question to photograph them side by side: the *dalang* courteously but firmly refused to confront them. This shows how very seriously these little *wayang* people are taken; as I said before, they are *not* just dolls to be trifled with.

These *wayang* stories were probably introduced to Java by the rulers of the Hindu dynasties and they became so deeply rooted in the people's culture that when they eventually embraced Islam (with its strict application of that part of the First Commandment which we, with our Greek heritage, have chosen to ignore, i.e. 'thou shalt not carve any graven image or make any human likeness, etc.'), they could not tear themselves away from their dearly loved puppets, even though so many of them consisted of their now abandoned gods. Perhaps the puppets looked more lifelike before the advent of Islam. Some people have suggested that the puppets' noses have been pulled and tweaked out of human semblance since the conversion in order to comply with the sterner new religion. Sumatra did not attempt to compromise, only Java, with its tolerance and infinite capacity for absorbing all creeds, succeeded in marrying the old with the new, but strict Javanese Muslims look askance at these relics of the more cheerful pagan times.

As is to be expected, the *kraton* puppets (they have two complete sets of over three hundred and sixty characters each) represent the most exquisite workmanship that has ever been lavished upon the little people; each one of them is a museum piece—but no, that is unfair comment and the puppets would object to it, I am sure; the very thought of being shut away in a museum would make them shiver for they lead a happy, pampered life in the *kraton*. How sorry they must feel for those of their colleagues who lie buried in the British Museum—a splendid institution, of course, but so gloomy, so far from the scent of frangipani trees and the light of the tropical sun!

I was shown the puppets—one unfinished—that had been fashioned by the first Sultan of Jogjakarta, and two figures of eighteenth-century soldiers, very fierce-looking with their waxed moustaches, which he must have cut out while in a playful, innovating mood.

'All the world's a stage and all the men and women merely players', wrote our great bard; a *dalang* might believe that he had been thinking of Javanese puppets when he composed that famous line, for a *wayang* performance is intended to be a symbol of the cosmos. The banana trunks on to which the puppets are pricked before the screen represent the surface of the earth where all creatures carry out their roles through the powers of the *dalang*. The puppets come to life under his influence and are therefore dependent upon him, but the *dalang* is also dependent upon the puppets, since he would not be able to fulfil his powers without them. In the same way, man is dependent upon God and God on man. Both complement each other.

Most *wayang* stories are based on variations of the age-old theme which dogs man from the cradle to the grave and which has inspired his profoundest dramas: the conflict between good and evil, the two principles upon which the world has been founded, and without which the world as we know it would not be possible. The first part of every *wayang* story portrays youth and its impetuosity; the second part shows the hero's growth and the development of reflection, and the third part: old age, with its accompanying insight and wisdom. The *dalang* spins out his tale in *kawi*, an ancient form of Javanese derived from Sanskrit, and, as I have already mentioned, this slow unfolding takes the best part of the night.

The first section that lasts from nine o'clock until midnight is casually called the 'introduction'; the second part, from midnight until three in the morning, involves the *wayang* characters in all manner of 'complications', while the last part—from three to six a.m.—brings the final solution or denouement with the victory of the 'good' party. This may be enthralling for those who can follow the complexities of *kawi*—indeed, it seems to produce a state of trance—but it is very difficult for Westerners, unlettered in old Javanese and used to fast-moving two- and three-hour shows at home, to refrain from falling asleep after (if not before) midnight.

Wayang performances have a basically mystic character. They are always given at night and while they last they are supposed to protect the audience from the influence of evil spirits. Special performances are always given on occasions such as a birth, birthdays, weddings, and promotions in rank—that is to say, at every important transitional period of a person's life.

The Sultan told me how a prophecy was made that the three *wayang* figures cut out by the first Sultan of Jogjakarta that had been dispersed (perhaps, who knows, during the English looting of the *kraton* in 1812) would be returned to the *kraton* in the reign of either the eighth or the ninth Sultan. Nothing happened in the lifetime of Hamengku Buwono VIII, but during the reign of the present Sultan—Hamengku Buwono IX—a Chinese merchant from Cheribon suddenly and unaccountably felt impelled to send one of the figures from his private *wayang* collection to the *kraton* of Jogjakarta. This was subsequently identified as one of the missing three. A little while later a farmer in Northern Java, whose house had been the only building spared in the kampong during a battle with the Dutch, was 'ordered' in a dream to send one of *his* puppets to the Sultan in Jogjakarta. This turned out to be the second of the *kraton's* lost puppets. The Sultan is now waiting confidently for the third puppet to be restored to him.

In a peeling white annexe off the now empty royal stables, *kraton* instructors teach the younger generation to fashion puppets in accordance with the exacting canons of a traditional art. The Prince took me to see them and we spent an afternoon following the different stages of their creations.

First, the outer form of the puppet is drawn upon leather and then the complete outline is cut with a chisel. There are twelve different chisel lines or motifs: the *tratasan*, in which short lines alternate with dots like a line of Morse (this alternation prevents the weakening of the puppets); the *untu walang* motif: a number of regular small stripes or teeth used for the edges of the kains, jackets, and breeches; the *bubukan* or chain, is used for the long pendant necklaces, a design of flower petals strung together fills in the ear and hair ornaments, a leaf design on symbols of rank is worn only by ruling princes in possession of their kingdom, and an imitation of gold-leaf work is used on diadems, the garuda shape used for holding the hair in place, and so on.

Although the puppets appear to be half-naked, their outfit consists of an astonishing number of items, all of which are most carefully chiselled and painted in: they range from ornamental collars, necklaces, waistbands, kains, apron plates, and straps, pendent tails of royal kains to long pants and ankle bracelets—the list is formidable. Connoisseurs can tell who is who at a glance. Gods wear long cloaks, a shawl, and footgear. Kings wear a special kind of pleated kain or *dodod* that sticks out like a bustle; warriors wear a *dodod* with a belt or pleat for the kris. There are three types of hair buns (the most characteristic is known as the 'lobster claw' from its shape). The facial colours can be red, white, gold, or black and the same individual may appear with one or the other colour according to his mood: black indicates calm and self-control; the coarsest characters have red faces and stand on the left of the screen while the noble, refined ones with black faces look towards the east.

The painting of the puppets' outfit is dictated by specific rules, for the Javanese say that every colour has its 'friendly' (i.e. complementary) colour: red and green, orange and blue, etc. When a puppet belongs to a grimacing type in which teeth and gums are visible, the teeth must be black. Crowns must always be red with brown shading along the edges and a blue top.

The 'finishing' is most important. This is called '*ambedah*', which means 'to break open', that is, to give life to a puppet by carving out its nose, mouth, and eyes. Eyes can be round, half-closed or—as in the case of priests and characters of high nobility—almost entirely closed. As you can see, *wayang* can hardly be described as child's play and I have not explained half its intricacies!

The *kraton wayang*-maker proudly showed us a fine specimen of the demi-god Bhima, who belongs to the Hindu epic of the Mahabharata and pointed out his characteristics: Bhima is a tyrannical type (although he always fights against evil). His massive limbs denote strength and his large nose indicates that he does not possess the 'inner refinement' of the others. He can always be recognized by his particularly large thumbnail which is a symbol of great self-control and he wears a chequered loincloth to show that he has undergone a mystical initiation. But not all of these *wayang* characters are so splendid and solemn—the Javanese are too fond of life and burlesque for that and they love to laugh at awkward Petruk and lazy Nalagareng, the jesting clowns and servants of Arjuna.

In the late afternoon, the Prince accompanied me to a *dalang* class, for the *kraton's* experts also instruct young men who come here from all over Java to be trained in the arduous profession of a *wayang* master of ceremonies. A *dalang* is expected to know many things: he must master old Javanese (as well as high and low modern Javanese); he must memorize the hundreds of complex *wayang* stories and modulate his voice to suit each character; he must know how to manipulate them and present them upon the screen in the manner appropriate to their rank; he must be conversant with *kraton* etiquette and be of a philosophical turn of mind; he must possess an excellent memory, a resonant voice, and enjoy good health, for he will be called upon to recite all night long without the aid of throat pastilles or intoxicating stimulants. To master these various accomplishments, the youthful aspirant will have to spend three years under the guidance of the *kraton's* professionals. He will have three teachers there: one for the spoken word, one for singing roles, and a third for the gamelan. He will not be required to pay more than a nominal fee of a few shillings a year, for the *kraton* of Jogjakarta still believes in art for art's sake.

When we went in, we found half a dozen *dalang* students squatting in the bare classroom to the right of the *wayang* screen. The teacher sat in the centre, immediately behind the pupil whose turn it was to manipulate the puppets in front of the screen, correcting him, making him repeat whole phrases—royal and jesting—as well as bursts of sarcastic clownish laughter, for they were rehearsing a scene in which a king who coveted another man's wife was engaged in a dialogue with his clown-counsellor. It was an ethical story and the clown was advising his royal master against taking steps to have his rival poisoned.

A full *wayang* performance was to be held on the following evening in one of the southern courtyards of the *kraton*. The Prince could not accompany me, for his wife had just given birth to a son, their eighth child. The parents had not yet thought of a name for the infant; they were waiting for inspiration, because the Javanese attach great importance to the bestowal of a name. The Prince's eldest son was called Tirunmarwita. *Marwita* means 'to become a Guru's pupil'. 'Let him come and talk to me when he grows older,' a wise old man asked the prince when the child was only nine years old, 'his insight is developed and he will understand much.'

This particular *wayang* performance was a regular monthly affair broadcast by the local radio station (the *kraton's* gamelan is likewise broadcast once a month by Radio Jogjakarta). My *betjak* boy actually seemed to know where to go for a change and when I directed him he plunged into the darkness with reckless determination. It was a very long, very dark ride through the high-walled streets behind the *alun-alun*, which are mysterious at all times and deserted at night. The *betjak* boy swerved left by the Water Palace and up a stately avenue of eucalyptus trees to a wide tropical baroque gateway (one of many similar ones that guard the various entrances to the *kraton*), but I had never seen this one before. It led to a courtyard and a pavilion in which a gamelan was marking time before the opening of the performance. The *betjak* boy suddenly became bashful and refused to penetrate into this inner sanctuary, leaving me to trip over the muddy ground as best I could.

It had begun to rain. In the dimly lit pavilion the *dalang* was seated beside his box of puppets, holding the *gunungan*, or pyramid-shaped mountain which is always set up in the middle of the screen before the puppets are 'brought to life' and begin their story. Timid tongues of flame, narrow as cats' tongues, quivered under the banyan trees. The menfolk were already gathered round the *dalang* inside the pavilion. I crossed over to a gateway opposite the screen to shelter from the rain under the wide overhang. From there I could see the shadowy puppets with their elongated, witch-like faces gesticulating with the only mobile limbs available to them: long thin arms charged with the *dalang's* emotional current. I sat on a low wall in front of an immense green gate flanked by red dragons. In the centre a gilded *makara* monster looked down with its bulging eyeballs and ugly leer upon the broadcasting engineers, intent upon the new magic of our age. They were surrounded by a large crowd of infant admirers—part of the regular contingent that haunt the *kraton* courtyards unchecked to gape at whatever happens to be going on at the time. Sometimes as noisy and troublesome as sparrows, they are easily hushed and always gravely enthralled by all that the *kraton* has to offer; outside school hours they grow up in a fairyland legacy of gamelan, *Srimpi*, and *wayang*. They live in an all-the-year-round pantomime atmosphere.

The rain sent up delicate currents from the soil, the residue of perfumes lavished upon it during the rites of many centuries. Two or three boys sauntered up to the banyan tree, sheath-like in their tightly-wound sarongs, smoking *kreteks*. Slender feminine figures crossed in front of the pavilion, their faces hidden behind bamboo parasols. Two radio men strutted up importantly in ill-fitting Western mackintoshes and caps. To my surprise, the show began punctually at nine o'clock and then dragged on endlessly, inexorably, like the tropical rain.

The modern *dalangs* of Djakarta are taking topical events into their stride too. For instance, the Bandung Conference, long since over, had been *wayangized* and was being shown at important adults' birthday parties. I do not imagine that the *dalangs* believe that they can ever compete with the newsreels, but in this case I think their instinct was sound. The Bandung Conference marked a turning-point in Asian—probably in world—history, and is therefore worthy of inclusion in the *wayang* repertoire. *Dalangs* are not concerned with transient daily news but with events likely to be remembered and discussed a long time afterwards. Yes, there is still life in the *dalang* profession and its members are still on their toes.

SECRETS OF THE REGALIA

THERE is a terrifying fascination about regalias. The finest craftsmen were employed to fashion them, the most splendid jewels were bought, presented, or plundered to enhance their value; but however boastfully they may glitter behind the glass and bars that protect them, they cast a sinister aura; magic and bloodshed are associated with every one of them. It has been so in Europe, as well as in the East, where stones and precious metals are alleged to possess occult qualities and to be inhabited by spirits incorporated by the artist-sorcerers who had them cut and chiselled. The *kraton* regalia of Jogjakarta is no exception. Only a portion of it remains, in souvenir of faded glories. I regret to have to say that the Sultan's finest diamonds were looted by English soldiers and later given to Raffles as a memento of their 'exploit' in sacking the palace. I do not know whether there was a curse placed upon them or not, but I daresay there must have been for none of the palace jewels are without some form of magic power. Every one of the rings that flashes upon aristocratic fingers possesses its guardian spirit and produces certain effects upon the wearer. Some, like a ring with a beryl in it, which can dissolve gallstones, are said to have healing powers.

Raffles did not keep his looted diamonds long, for they too were lost in the fire that destroyed all the valuable souvenirs of his four-year stay in the island. In December 1811, the Sultan Hamengku Buwono II, a 'turbulent and intriguing prince', wrote Crawfurd, wished to anticipate the events of 1945. He believed that the time was ripe for the expulsion of the Europeans, since the Dutch were involved in the Napoleonic wars and he refused to adhere to the treaty acknowledging the temporary sovereignty of the British over Java. So Raffles proceeded to Jogjakarta with a small escort of Light Dragoons to show him who was master, in the then still effective imperial way. When he reached the boundary of the Residency of Jogjakarta, he was met by multitudes of Javanese guards of honour, Crawfurd, and the Sultan. Carriages with four richly caparisoned horses were drawn up ready to drive his party to the capital, the finest of all being that reserved for the Sultan, at the top of the line. After the usual exchange of civilities, Raffles proposed to start for town and began to make his way to the first carriage. The Sultan, perceiving his object, pushed ahead but the English aides-de-camp kept him back while Raffles jumped into the first carriage with his officers and forced the coachmen and outriders to move on, surrounded by the British cavalry. The Sultan followed in a towering rage in the second carriage.

At Residency House in Jogjakarta, two golden thrones had been prepared for the distinguished visitors. The throne intended for Raffles stood slightly in front of the other. Raffles took his seat but the Sultan remained standing, declining to sit down until his throne was pushed forward. Raffles refused to allow this and a perfect uproar followed. Raffles unsheathed his sword, the Sultan drew his kris. It was a tense moment. Then Raffles quietly sheathed his sword while a few quiet words from Resident Crawfurd eased the tension and the Sultan was induced to sit down. (Incidentally, this Sultan had resumed government after putting to death his first minister and the latter's father for opposing his wishes.) When Raffles left the city the Sultan lost no time in forming a general confederacy of native courts and he even buried the hatchet with his hated rival the Emperor of Solo. Raffles heard of this and decided to move first; this time—June 1812—a real battle was fought in and around the *kraton*, which was bombarded and then plundered by the English. The old Sultan was banished to Penang and the hereditary prince mounted the throne at the age of nine, as Hamengku Buwono III. His regent appears to have been affable and the records of Raffles's third visit to Jogjakarta only mention how pleasantly the royal gamelans played along his route.

Undoubtedly the old Sultan was of a fiery and rather bloodthirsty disposition. He appears to have been firmly convinced of the divine mission of kings and of his own in particular. The more I ponder upon him the more convinced I become that he must have put a curse upon those diamonds because—like so many other Javanese rulers before him—he dabbled extensively in the occult arts.

I tried hard to find out what the court historians had had to say about Raffles, but I never succeeded. It must have been something so impolite that they did not dare to divulge the passages to me and thus mar the agreeable twentieth-century Anglo-Javanese relations between the Prince and myself. They did not realize that I would merely have been interested in their predecessors' account. It must exist somewhere, for everything that happens in the *kraton* is recorded in high Javanese verse and kept under lock and key by court chroniclers called *Widyo Budojo* and *Bandjar Wilopo*. On the other hand, it may well be that their filing system is faulty and that they simply could not lay their hands on the poems written during the frantic years 1811 and 1812.

In view of subsequent events—for Raffles proved that he was genuinely fond of the Javanese—and Indonesia's recent independence, I wonder whether the old Sultan's spirit has been moved to contrition? (After all, that diamond episode was a malicious piece of revenge which amounted to cutting his nose in spite of his face since so many manuscripts were sacrificed with them.) If so, was it he who made me dream about the mystic book he wrote during his lifetime? For one night in a dream I saw this book quite clearly and knew that it was kept in the *kraton*, that it was illustrated and filled with moral precepts and prophecies for the future Sultans of Mataram, prophecies that are coming true today. Since nobody had ever breathed a word to me about this book, the Prince was slightly taken aback when I questioned him upon the subject the next day. Apparently there is a curse on this book too, so that no one in the palace has dared to open it for years; it was removed from the library to the pavilion of heirlooms after three people in succession—one of them quite young—had died shortly after attempting to translate the manuscript into modern Javanese. I was assured that my dream had been quite accurate. The book *is* illustrated and the contents as I have described. When I was informed that it had been written by the second Sultan, I felt sure that the curse had now been lifted and that the time had come to reveal the book. This intuition was confirmed later by a Javanese mystic. What will happen now? Will the mysterious *Suriorojo*, meaning 'The Sun King', be divulged to the world? Apparently there are very few people with the necessary literary qualifications for such a task. The Sultan was informed of the incident and it is up to him to take a decision. He has the sense to believe in dreams, as people did in Biblical times with such good effect.

So, as I was explaining before this digression, the regalia of Jogjakarta has been stripped. It does not include what we would consider to be the main item of a regalia, namely, a crown. A Javanese crown is different from our conception of this regal adornment *par excellence*; it is like a winged fez, a form of head-gear resembling that worn by Egyptian Pharaohs. It is not made of any particularly durable substance and does not play an important part in the coronation ceremonial.

The various objects that compose the regalia are sacred and displayed to the public only once a year, when they are borne in procession to the *sitingil*, the 'high place', and arranged round the Sultan. Once a year, too, on the eve of the Muslim feast of the Idhul Adha (which fell on July 30th last year) the regalia is taken out by the *kraton* staff for a ceremonial cleansing. As a special favour, I was allowed to look at them and photograph them while they were being cleaned.

This operation was performed in a dark, dilapidated courtyard behind the Sultan's private apartments filled with unwanted bric-à-brac. Tall Victorian cupboards stood stiffly at attention behind curtains of cobwebs and rows of the same kind of blue and white flower-stands that adorned the late Sultan's offices were crammed together in the centre. Plants spilled out of them untidily—fiercely determined to live. The old Sultan had obviously had a craze for flower-stands which is not shared by his successor. Most objects are kept out in the open in Java; there are no attics as we know them and junk accumulates in odd corners of their gardens.

At the far end of this miniature courtyard the *kraton* staff—wearing the stoles that indicated they were handling royal possessions—sat around a large black tea kettle. Upon two trestle tables in front of them was a carefully laid collection of dazzling, delicately wrought insignia: a golden throne, footstool, and spittoon stood on the first table, and on the second a row of golden totems: a goose, stag, woodcock, peacock, snake, and hen; there were also a golden pyramid for the royal handkerchief, a make-up box, a golden bowl, and several fine krisses; scattered between these were heterogeneous objects such as a cowrie shell box from the eastern islands, a few empty cartridges and, of all things, a little worn knitted bag filled with marbles, which the third Sultan had played with when he was a child. Nobody seemed to know what they were doing there. Perhaps the little Sultan had left them there himself when he was watching the cleaning operation; these relics from the graveyard of childhood looked a little pathetic among all the gold. We fingered them thoughtfully, patted them and then gently laid them down again beside the solemn golden throne. In the meanwhile, the *kraton* staff continued to rub each object with lemon juice, sandalwood oil, and a special sort of nut, with frequent pauses for sips of tea between their exertions.

Even more sacred than the regalia are the *pusakas*, or royal heirlooms made up of swords and lances, that lie in a special pavilion called the *Probojekso*, at the bottom of enormous gilded coffers, wrapped between layers of *tchindé*—a red, yellow, and white printed Indian cotton to which the Javanese attach an almost religious significance. Once a year these *pusakas* are exhumed and brought out into the daylight to be cleaned by the Sultan's male relatives in the course of a special ceremony. The Sultan cleans the principal *pusaka* himself: this is the lance known by the name of *Kandjeng Kyahi Hageng Plèrèd*, whose secret history was revealed to me by one of the court chroniclers: a famous ascetic, Seh Maulana, was one day summoned to the assistance of a female hermit, Dewi Rasa Wulan, who discovered that she had become pregnant after having drunk from a forest pool. When she had given birth, Seh Maulana took the infant and gave it by way of consolation to a widow in a neighbouring village who had just lost a child. He also gave her a blade which grew into a lance and ultimately passed into the hands of a Prince of Mataram who wielded it successfully in war. His son used it to kill a hereditary enemy during a battle famous in the annals of Java.

The second most sacred *pusaka* is the sword *Kandjeng Kyahi Baru*, which was once the tongue of a snake. It was discovered in the branches of a banyan tree by a seer who presented it forthwith to the first Sultan of Jogjakarta. A third *pusaka*, a kris, is said to have been the gift of Prabu Yudistiro, one of the *wayang* figures.

Incense burns day and night in the *Probojekso*, where the sacred heirlooms are guarded by women old enough to have passed the menopause. Younger women are sometimes allowed to clean them, but not when they are menstruating. On the last occasion that the *pusakas* were removed for the annual purification ceremony, I was told that several of the assistants commented upon the arresting fragrance they exuded. The *pusakas* appear to be surrounded by the 'odour of sanctity' attributed in the West to the remains of certain saints.

Many Javanese continue to be guided by dreams, as I have had occasion to mention before, and they often have visions connected with those whom they revere, especially the Sultan. For instance, only a short while before my visit, a peasant came to Jogjakarta and requested an audience with the Sultan. He had had a dream, he said, in which he had been commanded to bring a white spearhead that had belonged to his family for generations and present it to the ruler of the *kraton*. He also had a black spearhead in the shape of a *wayang* figure with which he did not wish to part although in his dream he had received definite instructions to do so. After he had humbly presented the white spearhead to the Sultan, he suddenly fell at his feet in a fit. The Sultan in alarm ordered his servants to carry the man to an outer office where he was stretched out and his sarong loosened; at that moment the black spearhead fell to the ground and the Sultan wonderingly bent to pick it up. The instant he touched it the peasant recovered from his fit. When he realized what had occurred, he made a full confession of his sins of omission and went on his way after having left both spearheads with the Sultan as he had been instructed to do by the spirits.

A seer had recently informed the Sultan that if he wished to succeed in a certain venture, two people would have to be 'offered up'. The Sultan thought that these might be two of his cousins who had just died and been buried side by side. (Unlike Africa, however, human sacrifices have never been popular in Java.) But the seer said no, the victims had to be cocks of identical plumage and it would be a further excellent augury if a black hen could be found on the slopes of a certain mountain not far from Jogjakarta; the cocks were actually almost run over on a country road by one of the Sultan's brothers, who brought them back to the *kraton* as a curiosity and the black hen was found too, just as the seer had foretold. The fowl was black, the Sultan told me, even to its skin, and he had it placed in the *Probojekso* beside the holy *pusakas*. The hen died as the Sultan's first son was being brought into the world. The seer believes that this son is the incarnation of a former Sultan.

SUNLIGHT CEREMONY: 'MOUNTAINS OF FOOD'

MOST Javanese ceremonies take place early in the morning or late at night; in between these comparatively cool times the sun reduces his equatorial domains to silence and apathy, driving men and buffaloes into the languid twilight of coconut groves, except for the peasants for ever bending over their rice-fields under their umbrella hats like withered toadstools.

The *Idhul Adha* being a Muslim feast, the Masjumi (the moderate Mohammedan political party) had taken advantage of the occasion to organize a mass rally at 7 a.m. in the *alun-alun*. Thousands of their eager young followers turned up in snowdrop-fresh shirts by the side of their gleaming Dutch and British bicycles. All were dressed in their festive best; not a tear or stain or crease was to be seen . . . an extraordinary feat for such a poverty-stricken country. Sartorial displays on holy days in the countries between the Mediterranean and the equator are truly startling and put us to shame. Our 'Sunday best' is a poor show in comparison despite our superior financial means.

After the Masjumi oratory at the knobbly feet of the banyan trees, the white-shirted youths dispersed and made way for ambling family groups and chirping toy-vendors; bright sarongs turned towards the mosque and gorgeous balloons in the shape of birds and dragons floated serenely heavenwards.

I hurried past scores of interesting sarong patterns, evidently reserved for feast days, to keep my appointment with the Prince in the *kraton* courtyard adjoining his office, where the traditional 'mountains of food' were waiting to be carried to the mosque. I found the courtyard thronged with people, mostly excited children; among them was the Prince's ten-year-old daughter. She was dressed in a short Western-style frock with a pink bow in her hair and had dancing brown eyes in a pretty, heart-shaped face;

kampong and *kraton* children were jumbled up together, united in a common eagerness to secure a good view of the splendid 'mountains' set up beside the pavilion; these were being gravely and incongruously guarded by tough policemen in khaki uniforms and white helmets who looked for all the world like ex-guerrilla fighters. The whispering, chuckling children advanced between their legs and then retreated—like the pigeons in Trafalgar Square—not quite sure as to what lengths the policemen were prepared to go in order to preserve the space round the traditional *kraton* 'mountains'. They eyed me enviously as I stepped forward with the Prince and walked round the brilliant pyramids so artistically decorated with red chillies, green beans, and rainbow-hued rice flowers.

The tallest *gunungan* or 'father mountain', headed the line; behind him was his pregnantly rounded 'wife' and close to her was the smallest of the three *gunungans*, their 'offspring'. Each one was laid upon a wooden platform through which poles had been slung; the two serried rows of *kraton* attendants who would be escorting them to the mosque squatted upon the polished floor, hieratic and impassive, the indigo blue of their sarongs reflected upon their sombre faces. Their presence served as a check to unseemly mirth, a reminder that this was no saturnalian carnival, but an echo from fetish cults of the distant past. No orgiastic drumbeats are ever heard in Java. The ceremonious procession to the mosque is only a diplomatic façade, a *mariage de raison* between colourful paganism and austere Islam characteristic of Java. Both the Javanese and the Spanish are the most ingenuous peoples in the world when it comes to the religious whitewashing of their old heathen feast days.

These cheerful *gunungans* festooned with the products of Mother Earth preceded Islam by hundreds of years; they, together with the *wayang* mountain, represent the earth and the Tree of Life (already depicted in Assyrian sculpture of the ninth century B.C.). They are our Christmas Tree and Maypole, hung with offerings, rich in blessings . . . the symbol of all that sprouts from the fertile soil. When the *kraton* was more affluent (and the peasants no

148

poorer than they are today) the *gunungans* were bigger and richer too; they were escorted by mounted palace guards in striking uniform who fired guns on their way to the mosque. In the old days too the peasant farmers would flagellate their cattle and beat their rice-fields with whips to ensure fertility. (Is our own springtime 'beating of the bounds' a distorted version of this custom, I wonder?)

Somebody, somewhere, gave the signal for the procession to start; the attendants scrambled on to their feet and the children sent up a delighted cheer as they advanced towards the *gunungans* and began to carry them shoulder-high out of the pavilion. Behind the three *gunungans* came other food offerings arranged on plates and borne upon trays covered with a white cloth like corpses; they were to be presented to the Imam and other mosque officials; even the police force came in for their share of goodies, although it was difficult to imagine that they ever enjoyed anything of a carnal nature.

Children and adults surged forward and we were whirled away on the crest of a happy human wave, through the three-tiered pagoda-shaped gateway, across the *alun-alun*, where we were joined by more crowds, under the banyan trees and cages of round-eyed *perkututs* to the left, through another gateway into the peaceful courtyard, past the pink-roofed palace mosque and into the small, private domain of the white-robed Imam and his assistants who sat huddled together like prophets, with their backs turned to the seductive world of sunshine, jasmine, and rose-throated doves that wafted scent and songs over them with subtle tropical insistence.

They did not even turn to look at us when we arrived, flushed and triumphant, after battling with the police at the entrance who at first failed to recognize the Prince and scowled at us discouragingly. The children were finally shooed off, the great door quivered, the *gunungans* were marched through and finally set down beside the pavilion of the white-robed figures; there was a tumult behind the door and the distant sound of gamelan and boogie-woogie records in obstinate competition in the *alun-alun*.

A long decorous Javanese pause followed during which the bearers sorted themselves out, the corpse-like trays were conveyed inside the pavilion, and everybody waited until the prophets condescended to give signs of returning to life. They unfroze very gradually, and slowly turned their heads towards the gifts; then one of them stretched out a bony, inquiring hand and hooked one of the trays that had been placed beside him. He lifted a corner of the white cloth, while the other prophets peered intently at the contents underneath; another tray slid forward discreetly. As the prophets began to gesticulate and to murmur their appreciation, the Imam nodded to an attendant with an air of superior resignation intimating that now the mob could be let in. They were hammering at the gates like British football fans. When it was opened, they streaked in like a flow of lava and hurled themselves upon the *gunungans*. In a few seconds the mountains were plucked and stripped to their bamboo frames: children and peasants from outlying kampongs chattered like monkeys, their arms full of rice-cakes and sweets. The peasants would proudly hang their trophies up in their homesteads that evening, confident that they would bring them luck and plentiful crops for at least a year.

MOONLIGHT CEREMONY:
IN THE SULTANS' CEMETERY

IF you were to float over the island of Java from the south by helicopter any Thursday evening, you would be intrigued by the number of lights—no bigger than glow-worms from the air—flickering along the coast, through jungle paths, upon the hills, and especially one hill sixteen miles west of Jogjakarta. And if curiosity prompted you to land you would be surprised to find that those lights were being carried by quiet streams of pilgrims on their way to and from a popular shrine. The lights on the hill to the west of Jogjakarta dance to the skies in honour of the Sultans of Mataram who lie in the royal cemetery of Imogiri.

Tongues of flame, tongues of hissing serpents embodied in royal krisses, black and white cockerels found upon volcanic slopes, hens with black skins that die when a royal heir is born, mystics in meditation beside ancient tombstones . . . all the occult and hair-raising magic of Java is to be found upon Imogiri on a Thursday night when the moon is riding high and Chief Merapi contentedly puffs up smoke from the crater of his immense wigwam. This is the time to be astir if you wish to sniff the essence of Java's aging, cosmic soul. Man has lived upon this steamy volcanic soil for thousands of years. The oldest remains of human bones have been unearthed, quite recently, along the banks of the Solo river only a few miles away from here. For how many aeons have flames risen towards invisible spirits from these hills and shores? One's brain reels at the very thought.

We left the *kraton* for Imogiri in the useful palace jeep and followed a bumpy, dusty road. The peasants are used to these bad roads and their hardy feet do not even notice the roughness of the surface. They always tread and sleep close to the bosom of the earth and do not find her hard. Even chimpanzees make themselves more comfortable for the night than the peasants of Java.

At Imogiri, we got out of the jeep and plunged into the darkness in the direction of the stone terraces and the three hundred and forty-five steps that lead up to the cemetery on the hill. Fortunately, the Prince had brought an electric torch with him, for the moon was constantly entangled in cloud. We climbed barefoot, to conform to tradition; the stones were still warm from the day's sun. Ghostly figures glided up and down on each side of us; most of them were silent but when they spoke it was in whispers. From a long way off, we could see the orange glow of offerings at the top of steps that leaned against the sky like an enormous ladder.

The entrance to the cemetery was closed but Sultan Agung's tiered mausoleum was easily distinguishable in the centre; it was chiefly for him that the incense was burning so brightly on the upper stone terrace. Ultimately, we found ourselves sandwiched between two separate groups of ancestor-worshippers; behind the shrub in front of us sat a band of exclusively female devotees. One person in each group had charge of the incense bowls which were stirred from time to time until delicate outstretched hands pressed more scented packets into the flames. The simpler-minded among the peasant folk petitioned the Sultans of yore for worldly benefits; others, deep in meditation, endeavoured to unite with his spirit.

A wind shivered waif-like between the palms and twisted the crackling flames towards the massive grey tiers. Only the wind and the flames and an occasional whisper disturbed the immense, joyful stillness of the night. Many of the pilgrims would be staying here until the dawn, praying and dreaming prophet-like dreams shot through with symbols and riddles. Few of them noticed the presence of the Prince and of his foreign guest; those who did soon turned away, for they had not come here to gossip. Nobody ate or drank or slept. This was a genuine Javanese pilgrimage, highly unorthodox as far as Islam is concerned. In the courts of justice of Jogjakarta men have been known to take the oath in the name of 'the Javanese religion'. For many of these, the *wayang* is equivalent to a holy book, and they respectfully refer to God as 'the greatest *dalang* of all'.

LIFE IN THE *KRATON*

A GREAT flame-coloured bird came swooping towards us as we sat under the cream trumpets of a frangipani tree, where the Prince was talking to me about palace life. With its wide outspread wings and noble, gilded beak it was indeed a worthy replica of Garuda, that combination of eagle and supernatural roc, transposed from Hindu mythology to Javanese *wayang orang*. Now another bird came bursting through the foliage; this one was as vividly green as young rice-shoots and wore a grinning mask. Each bird bore a prince upon its back, naked to the waist, dusted with yellow powder, gleaming with golden diadems, earrings, griffons, and pendants of a similar design to those of the leather puppets.

These splendid creatures were from the *kraton's* theatrical troupe to which members of the Sultan's family also belong (Prince Prabuningrat has often acted in *wayang orang* performances), and today they were rehearsing for a special performance which was shortly to be presented to V.I.P. guests outside the *kraton*. The Prince asked whether I would like to see the troupe's wardrobe, and soon we were climbing up a wooden staircase in a building adjoining the court ladies' apartments. At the top, a fantastic world: half-dream, half-nightmare, was revealed—a world of pantomime raised to the status of drama, of ghostly battles and snarling spirits, innumerable hero-kings and their bejewelled ladies. Here was a glass cabinet filled with crowns and diadems and another packed with *kebayas* in velvet, silk, and brocade, and masks set out like trophies of a titanic battle between demons. The corridors glittered with caparisoned apocalyptic steeds and monsters: Eastern Calibans from phantom Chambers of Horrors.

It was good to see the sunlight again outside, where a few of the Sultan's children were playing together in the garden beside their mothers' apartments. Each one of the Sultan's three wives (who are aristocrats of the *Buyot* or third rank, according to the *kraton's* complex hierarchy of nineteen different grades of nobility) has her own separate house and the Sultan, faithful to Koranic precept on this thorny subject, sleeps with each wife in turn and in strict rotation. The fruits of these royal beds are charming and alert; very democratically they go to school outside the *kraton* with the other children of Jogjakarta. Will the present Sultan end by having as many children as his predecessors? This would appear to be unlikely for the *kraton* population is on the decrease; the Sultan's grandfather had seventy-five children, but his father left only twenty-nine.

Several interesting rites connected with infants—both in anticipation of their birth and afterwards—are observed in the *kraton*.

When a woman is seven months' pregnant she endeavours to influence her future child's physical appearance in the course of a special ceremony. For this, worm-shaped images of the foetus are fashioned from rice-flour. The silhouettes of Janiko and his wife, the handsomest pair in the *wayang* repertoire, are carved in outline upon two young coconuts which are cut open during a *slametan* for the mother to drink the contents of both. This ensures that her baby will be as fine as Janiko if it is a boy or as beautiful as his wife if it turns out to be a girl.

When a baby is born in the *kraton* the afterbirth is carefully buried in a special part of the grounds reserved for this important object connected with the life of the spirit. The mother must then remain indoors for forty days. That was why only two of the Sultan's wives were accompanying him to his hillside villa at Kaliurang on the following Sunday; the third wife had just given birth to a son and was still confined to her apartments.

When a baby is seven months old, the 'touching the ground' ceremony takes place. (This is practised by kampong people as well as by the *kraton*, for these two poles of society are the greatest sticklers for tradition.) The purpose of the ceremony is to formally introduce the new babe to the all-powerful Mother Earth from whom it has issued and to whose broad bosom it will eventually return. Dust to dust. . . .

The babe's soft body is rolled over with moist balls of clay in the seven colours of the rainbow, and ritually bathed; then it is gently lowered to the ground in a large bamboo cage. Beside it in the cage are placed a live hen, or feathers, grains of rice, coins, and a golden chain. Whichever of these objects the tiny fingers touch first will determine the infant's future fate. A Javanese friend told me for instance that her brother had touched the feathers first when he was a baby so that none of his family were surprised when later he became a pilot in the Indonesian Air Force!

The next important stage in life is reached at puberty when adulthood is in sight and childish toys must soon be put away. Male circumcision is practised in Java as in all Mohammedan countries, but I do not think it is generally known that female circumcision—the excision of the clitoris as practised in Africa—is performed at the *kraton*. A special room in the *kraton* is reserved for these circumcision rites which take place between the ages of fifteen and seventeen for boys and twelve for girls (before the first menstruation). Both boys and girls are fed on a diet of dry food for several days before the operation which nowadays is performed with the aid of an anaesthetic, and by palace experts. The boy or girl to be operated upon climbs on to a four-poster bed enveloped by a mosquito net, which symbolizes the 'forest' of the inexperienced in search of his or her way through life; behind the net the bed is piled high with cushions covered with red, yellow, and white printed *tchindé* cotton, where an elder uncle or aunt (according to the child's sex) is waiting to receive its head upon their lap and to pass their hands lightly over its eyes during the operation. This represents the guiding function of wise old age, helping youth on to the path of life.

Some Javanese fathers, like their Spanish counterparts, are so afraid of their sons developing abnormal sexual habits that they bundle them off to brothels from their teens so that they may acquire 'the right kind of experience'. (They would be horrified to hear of our Public School 'tarts'!) Sex life begins early in these exuberant countries and Javanese males proudly claim that they have no use for aphrodisiacs.

*   *   *   *

Passing to affairs of the palate, I must mention two exquisite fruit beverages which have been preserved in the *kraton*. They are ignored by the 'moderns' outside, where teetotal Muslims indulge in a revolting synthetic 'orange krush' of which goodness knows how many gallons *per capita* are consumed every year in Indonesia. Somebody must be making a fortune. And yet the islands, with their wealth of fruits and spices, have developed elixirs comparable in distinction to the delicacy of gamelan music and of the Javanese language. These subtle, spicy flavours, like all that is really worth while in Java, are to be found both in the kampongs at the edge of the jungle and—developed to a royal degree—in the *kraton*. These amber-coloured liquids are called respectively *Chamu-param* and *Bumba Bir*. The royal chef, informed of my enthusiasm, was kind enough to divulge the recipe of the latter. It filled an entire sheet of foolscap paper and was signed with a justifiable flourish. There are over fifteen ingredients in this ambrosia, none of which—with the exception of ginger—are available in England.

Perhaps one day I shall decide to start importing spices on a grand scale and launch *Bumba Bir* bars in London. The name alone should attract countless bouncing customers. Perhaps the *Bumba Bir* era will supplant the present rage for Espressos and ultimately extend even to Java, whose Westernized middle class looks with disdain upon many a pleasant Eastern product.

*   *   *   *

I have referred to the subtlety of the Javanese language, but in the *kraton* it is particularly refined for not only are 'high' and 'low' forms of Javanese spoken there, but in addition *bagongan*, or 'middle' Javanese, which is peculiar to the palace. This 'middle' language is spoken in the presence of the Sultan. Outside the palace he is always addressed in 'high' Javanese. When he is not present, 'low' Javanese is spoken with the servants. There is quite a difference between these various forms. I will give you just one example (to be candid, it is the only one I know): 'That is a dog' is rendered by *Kui asu*, in 'low' Javanese, by *Meniko segawon* in 'high', and by *Puniko segawon* in 'middle' Javanese. Such complexities make one thankful to be English. Javanese, as Resident John Crawfurd so aptly remarked, is 'a language of deference'. That is probably one of the reasons why the egalitarians (in theory) of the new Republic have chosen the far simpler and more direct Malay idiom, which has always been the archipelago's *lingua franca*, for their official language. 'To express the different modifications of sound, there are not less than fifty words in Javanese,' wrote Crawfurd ecstatically. '*Gumrot*, for instance, signifies the noise of a door on its hinges, while *gunret* and *gumrit* express the same thing in a less intense degree. There are also ten ways of standing and twenty ways of sitting and each has its distinct and specific appellation.'

★　　★　　★　　★

It is considered a great honour, all over the Indonesian archipelago, to be related to the *kraton* dynasty and distant relations—both literally and figuratively—turn up at the palace gates every week to have their credentials vetted by the palace specialist whose sole but considerable task in life consists in keeping family trees up to date. Since many of the Sultans and their relatives were banished to the outer islands at various periods in the colonial history of Indonesia for having conspired against the alien occupier, it is obvious that the royal family has sown its seed far and wide. That is why their descendants, when they can afford to make the journey, come from Macassar in the Celebes, from Banda and Sumatra, bringing a witness with them and a sheaf of documents. (An odd assortment. They cannot be birth certificates because until recently the Javanese were not in the habit of keeping civil registers, nor did they have consistent surnames from father to son. This confusion is now being tidied up.) Those were the people I had seen sitting in the porch before the Prince's office upon my first visit. Every Thursday morning claimants to *kraton* titles are interviewed and endless discussions and investigations are entered into before they are given a certificate proving their connection with the palace. At times as many as three hundred applicants have to be dealt with in a week. Some of them are humble folk who find that it is of enormous prestige value to have been related to a *kraton* cook or gardener.

The 'divine aura of kings' extends to everybody and everything that surrounds the Sultan. Yes, everything—even to the water with which his carriages are washed down each week. The people of the town and from outlying kampongs gather beside the gates to collect this washing water and to bathe their faces in it, believing—like the English maidens who immersed their faces in dew on Midsummer mornings—that it will make them comely. It is the water that serves to wash *Nyai Jimat* that is thus coveted. *Nyai Jimat* is the most baroque of all the Sultan's coaches, with a gilded female form in front to which people bring the traditional offerings reserved for shrines: rose petals and pandan leaves. The mercenary elements among them sell this washing water from *Nyai Jimat*, which is subsequently used by witch doctors in their black magic recipes.

A JAVANESE PRINCESS GETS MARRIED

A MARRIAGE had been arranged between Raten Ageng Sitisuharti, a twenty-year-old princess of the second degree *kraton* aristocracy, and a twenty-three-year-old Captain in the Indonesian Air Force. Prince Prabuningrat accompanied me behind the scenes to watch the unfolding of the traditional ceremony which in princely weddings such as this proceeds step by step at the ritualistic tempo of a *Srimpi* dance. Most of the outward forms are relics of the colourful Hindu period but the actual marriage contract is drawn up according to Muslim law. The frills belong to a creed with more imagination and sense of drama which lingers on wherever it can to enliven the uneventful routine of Javanese life.

The Princess was an orphan who had spent all her young life within the walls of the *kraton*; but a few days before the wedding she had moved to the house of an aunt—in the shadow of the Water Palace—after having first obtained the Sultan's consent to her marriage and ceremoniously kissed his knee before her departure, to conform with court etiquette.

Since neither the Princess nor any of the *kraton* ladies could speak English, Prince Prabuningrat escorted me to their private apartments where the esoteric preparations were being made and, as usual, he acted as my interpreter. He was the only male present among a bevy of young girls and a formidable array of aunts.

Although I did not know the number of the house in which the ceremony was to be held, my *betjak* boy soon found it. He pedalled slowly down the street looking for the 'wedding signs' —a front pavilion decorated with coconuts, banana trees, and paddy stalks. The Prince was already waiting for me and we inspected the decorations before going inside. The cleft banana trees with their downward-hanging fruit and coconuts tied behind them were realistic symbols of fertility. The bananas were of the *pisang raja* variety, signifying that the bridal pair were to be the king and queen of the show. Paddy stalks are a sign of prosperity.

From the pavilion, which was being filled by the servants with rows of chairs as for a concert, leaving a space at the end for the gamelan players, we passed into a sombre anteroom. Here we left our shoes and stepped on to the platform where the bridal settee was being protected by burning incense and offerings to the *Dewas* or angels. An assortment of fetish-like objects were placed at its stumpy feet: little pyramids of rice mixed with red chillies (like miniature 'mountains of food'), bowls of rose petals and a gruesome buffalo head which had only recently been severed from its body, stuck without ceremony in a pail; the raw, suppurating neck was packed with coarse salt to preserve it and prevent the smell from becoming too overpowering. A buffalo head is considered to be a good luck talisman all over Indonesia. It is also often buried on the site of a new building. This is still done—even in Djakarta.

Behind this anteroom lay the bedchamber in which the bride would spend her last night as a virgin. This is called the 'night of the angels' when doors are left open for the angelic hosts who depart at dawn after having showered their blessings through the night. The bride's young friends keep her company as she sits or reclines upon a mattress placed on the floor to prevent her from falling asleep. It is probably intended that the bride should be naturally 'doped' by the time she is ready to submit to her groom's embraces on the following night; this seems to be sound psychology in Javanese circumstances, and it must help to mitigate virginal shock.

The bride, her friends, and a sallow background of aunts were squatting on the floor, doing nothing in particular. We soon kept them busy answering our questions. Our principal informant was the eldest aunt, a rather awesome lady in spite of her slight figure, whom everybody politely salaamed, even the Sultan's eldest sister, before they began to speak to her and then again when they had finished speaking to her—a most tedious point of etiquette to have to follow. The Prince had to submit to this custom too.

The bride looked utterly dejected, although she must have been seething with excitement inwardly. This is part of Javanese facial etiquette; they are supposed to look composed, even indifferent, on the most important occasions of their life, and marriage is one of them. Until the ceremony is over the bride is bound to look timid and miserable. I felt indecently cheerful, but both the Prince and his sister were equally good-humoured and nobody objected to our many exchanges of pleasantries. The bride continued to pout while we played the role of reporters, to the amusement of the young people present. She was plump for a Javanese, with small features and a rosebud of a mouth. Most of the time she remained mute and restrained in her gestures and sat watching us, scarcely conscious that she was the centre of attraction—a perfect example of a *kraton*-bred young Javanese girl. Within less than a week she would be living in the tumult of Djakarta, free to go about as she pleased. How I should like to meet her again in two years' time, on my next visit, to see what marriage and freedom have done to her!

This room too was filled with charms and offerings. The four-poster in the alcove was draped with red, black, and yellow strips of *tchindé* cotton to avert evil spirits. Tufts of banana leaves and paddy stalks were nailed to the walls. The bamboo mat upon which we were sitting was strewn with rose petals, pandan leaves, and grains of rice. A row of incense bowls and plates of foodstuff were arrayed against the wall to the back of us; from time to time, the live chicken tightly imprisoned in a bamboo bag in the corner rustled with impatience and discomfort as it vainly endeavoured to stretch its cramped legs.

Servants crept up in the deferential *dodok* posture, like injured crabs, to revive us all with tea and cakes. They, and the cooks in charge of meals, were wearing the *sindur*, a red cotton waistband edged with white—specially designed to frighten malevolent spirits that might feel tempted to tamper with the wedding food, for it is a well-known fact that the powers of evil are particularly active when important ceremonies are about to take place.

The bride too was wearing a special waistband of white cotton, with a piece of string tied underneath to signify that she had the same rights as her husband-to-be. She wore a sarong of a unique wedding-eve pattern with small circles (intended to represent harmony), stylized birds, fish scales, deer heads, and a trilobular motif round the edges.

The time had come for the ritual bath and the eldest aunt led the bride, two attendants, and myself into the Malay-type bathroom which led off an adjoining parlour lined with glass cabinets; some of these were filled with sarongs and others with china. One of them was reserved for the wedding presents. For once, the Prince had to be left behind. In any case, no interpreter was required in the bathroom, for the performance was entirely visual and no explanation was needed.

The bride was seated upon a stool in a white cotton wrap wound under her armpits. First her long black hair was loosened and rinsed by her aunt from an earthenware jar filled with water in which rose petals had been strewn. Her face too was carefully bathed in this water. Now the aunt took a saucer upon which were placed seven little balls of a creamy substance coloured blue, pink, red, green, yellow, white, and orange. (These are similar to the balls with which the seven-months-old baby is rubbed before the 'touching the ground' ceremony.)

The aunt kneaded the balls together with an experienced hand until they dissolved into a blue mass and then she daubed the bride's face, breast, and back. The blue lather was washed off immediately afterwards with modern toilet soap and after a final rinse with the rose-petal water, the aunt hoisted the empty earthenware jar shoulder-high and hurled it against the opposite wall, where it broke into a dozen jagged pieces. The exact meaning of each separate phase of this ritual bath has been forgotten, but the overall purpose of it is to 'bring out the glitter of the bride just as the meteorite in a kris shines when it has been cleaned with lemon juice'.

The bridegroom had arrived from Djakarta three days before, but it is considered very unlucky for a young couple to see each other before the wedding day. That evening he came to the pavilion of the house where the bride was staying to sign the wedding contract. The bride never appeared. She was represented by her uncle who was as tubby as the *kraton rakshashas*. On the previous evening, officials from the local Department of Religious Affairs had called upon the bride to ascertain whether she had in any way been coerced into the betrothal. The same officials now returned to ask the same odd question of the groom, who looked like a Persian prince rather than a captain in the air force, with his silk turban and splendid plume. He appeared to be a good-natured, rather shy young man. The religious officials in white drill suits and black *pitchis* sat round the table and proceeded to ask him the strangest questions. Did he knew that his future bride was an orphan? Would he promise not to beat her, or to leave her alone for more than six months at a time? If he did, they informed him, his wife would have the right to appeal to the Department of Religious Affairs. After the symbolic 'wedding gold'—a token sum of five rupiahs—had been submitted by the groom, a beautifully bound copy of the Koran was presented on his behalf to be given to the bride; prayers were recited for the welfare of the newly-wed, refreshments were served, then the groom's car rolled up the drive and off he went back home.

The Prince met me again just before noon on the following day to watch the bride being made up for the evening ceremony, when she would at last confront the groom. This make-up was as elaborate as for a *wayang orang* performance, with the same colourful but highly theatrical results.

When we arrived, we found the bride squatting in the parlour upon an auspicious bundle of five different kinds of leaves and five squares of cotton: green, red, yellow, blue, and white. Incense was burning and rice offerings had been placed in bowls round the room. A battalion of aunts was massed in the background. The make-up expert from the *kraton*, who had just come from a similar operation on the bridegroom's face, squatted in front of the placid bride, surrounded by jars, boxes, tins, bottles, and trays of trinkets. This expert, a middle-aged woman with a bright, intelligent face, set about her task with a self-confident air. After a little while, the Prince, his sister, and I had a much-needed break for lunch in the back pavilion, returning to note the progress made in our absence.

The bride's hair was dealt with first; this was the longest part of the performance. Five triangles were outlined in carbon black round the bride's forehead and then filled in with a thick greasy mixture of carbon black and oil until they were indistinguishable from her own hair, which had been brushed up into a tight bun at the top of her head. An edging of tiny pieces of gold leaf was pressed round the triangles. This operation took two hours. Then a gold motif in the shape of a crown was fixed on the bun, and a garland of white *melatti* flowers wound round it falling in scented strings at the nape of her neck; a golden dragonfly was impressed upon her forehead on a wax background and an enamelled coating of paint and powder completed the transformation of the demure little Javanese princess into an exotic puppet. Her eyes were heavily underlined and prolonged by upward slanting strokes of the brush. Immense earrings were suspended from her shell-like ears; quivering golden flowers on pins were stuck into her hair; finally, she was arrayed in a hereditary wedding costume: a gold-leaf printed sarong, a crimson velvet long-sleeved jacket embroidered with gold thread. Jewels and golden chains were endlessly entwined round her neck. She was not allowed to admire the stiff splendour of her wedding raiment. Again according to inexorable custom all the mirrors in the house had been covered so that she should not see her reflection in them until the wedding was over, for that would have been unlucky.

At seven o'clock the gamelan began to play cautious, whispering tunes in the front pavilion. The guests arrived and filled the seats—the men on the gamelan side, the ladies in the loggia opposite, separated by a width of drive where an interesting variety of vehicles drew up to disgorge the bridegroom and his best men from shiny black limousines; they were followed by a file of sheathed figures who jumped nimbly off jeeps and high-wheeled yellow buggies. Nobody cheered the bridegroom, although he really should have got a round of applause. I thought he had looked impressive the night before but tonight, *wayangized* like his bride, he was truly magnificent and not quite of this world—a Prince Charming in an Eastern décor. What a pity there would be no dancing, no champagne, and no laughter!

As the groom stepped out of his limousine, an attendant rushed forward to hold a golden parasol over him while he slowly advanced towards his seat in the centre of the pavilion. He wore a gold-leaf sarong, an embroidered jacket, a tall black and gold Javanese crown corresponding to the rank of *Bupati*; garlands of flowers and leaves fell from his ears to his waist and *melatti* flowers were draped over his kris. (This sartorial custom dates from the sixteenth century when a famous prince by the name of Ario Penangsan had his abdomen cut open during a battle; in order to continue the fight, he wound his entrails round the handle of his kris—he died unsheathing this kris, which is preserved among the sacred heirlooms in the *Probojekso*.) His face was pink and cream, his eyes almost as heavily made up as his bride's—and lowered with captivating modesty. We sat quite close to him, the Prince and I, at a little table decorated with Scorpion orchids.

As the last vehicle moved off the servants advanced with a plain yellow wooden box which they placed on the ground between the loggia and the pavilion, with an earthenware vessel full of water and a silver ladle beside it. While this was going on, trays of refreshments were passed round to the hundreds of guests; each one contained five meat balls, five sweet balls, and two boiled sweets wrapped in paper. (I noticed—for we had plenty of time on our hands—that one of the sweets came from a Dutch firm while the other hailed all the way from Hull in England.)

The gamelan began to strike the gongs more loudly and broke into the 'sirih leaf tune' as the bride emerged from the house between two attendants, with her head meekly bowed as for a sacrifice. The groom and his attendants rose and advanced towards her until the two groups stood confronting each other —one in each pavilion. The attendants of both groom and bride handed them packets of sirih leaves which they playfully proceeded to throw at one another; the object of this was to discover which of the two—whoever was 'struck' first—would become the dominating partner in the new household. The bride's attempts were half-hearted—it looked as though she would prove to be a submissive wife. Then the groom descended the three steps leading from the pavilion to the drive, stepped out of his sandals, and stood inside the wooden box. One of the aunts made a pretence of assisting the bride to lift a ladle-full of water (for she is supposed to appear to be reluctant to do this herself) and pour it over his bare feet. One of the groom's assistants threw an egg into the box, which broke at his feet, thus adding to his discomfort. This symbolized the 'blending of seeds', unity and fertility. While the groom stepped back into his sandals, the bride advanced towards him, shuffling round the box with tiny hesitating steps; timidly extending her left hand, they clasped their little fingers together and walked slowly up to a white settee in the centre of the loggia. Here they sat side by side, with a sarong wrapped round both of them to symbolize their unity, silent— their faces as blank as masks, aloof as demi-gods. After a pause, they stood to receive the files of guests who pressed forward to congratulate them and wish them happiness. The Prince hastily taught me an appropriate phrase in Javanese to which the groom replied: 'Thank you very much,' in excellent English.

The young couple's ordeal was not yet over. Half an hour later, they drove to the other end of the town, to the house in which the groom was staying, where they were to spend the night. Here too a settee was waiting for them (this time, it was an old-fashioned red plush one). It was a warm night and the poor young couple must have been suffering torments under their heavy paint and weighty clothes. The Sultan's children tiptoed in, full of well-behaved eagerness and his two eldest daughters, in short pink frocks and black pigtails, took up their position on either side of the resplendent bridal pair and proceeded to fan them—an act of charity for which they must have felt deeply grateful.

After another decorous pause, the couple rose—the bride still sheepishly hanging her head—and proceeded to the nuptial chamber which was buzzing with aunts; the Prince and I slipped through them like a couple of eels and seated ourselves on the floor of the tiny bedroom for there were still two more scenes to be enacted before the bedroom door was shut in our face—two little scenes to be played before close relatives only.

The bridegroom sat on the edge of the bed (after the mosquito net had been lightly pulled aside) on the pale blue mattress. The pillows behind him were also pale blue and the mosquito net was decorated with leaves and flowers; altogether it looked like a huge cradle. A paper poke full of coins and coloured rice-wafers like large confetti was pressed into his hand; the bride then squatted at his feet, with a cloth spread over her knees. The groom poured his rice and coins into her lap . . . had she let any of them fall out-side it would have meant that she was going to be an extravagant housewife. Two of the bride's aunts gathered up the cloth of coins while other aunts—she had an unlimited supply at her dis-posal—escorted her towards the 'supper' laid out on a spotless tablecloth upon the floor. The groom joined her and they squatted side by side, slightly more relaxed now, since only the family were present. One of the aunts pushed a plateful of rice in front of the groom; he stretched out his right hand and made a gallant attempt to knead five little balls out of the rice to present to his wife, but it should have been of a firmer consistency for the grains would not stick together. The Prince and I murmured words of sympathy from the opposite side of the tablecloth while the groom struggled valiantly; the bride giggled and the groom turned towards her with a pleased smile at this first indication of humanity from her, then he helped to put a fork and spoon in her hands after she had helped herself to some *sambel* (chilli sauce) to make the dissolving rice-balls more palatable. This little comedy indicates that the dutiful wife is prepared to accept whatever her husband has to offer her in the course of their married life. It is a gastronomic interpretation of: 'for better or for worse.'

A few weeks later in Djakarta, I met the newlyweds strolling happily arm-in-arm admiring the foreign pavilions at the International Trade Fair. Prince Charming in an open-necked shirt, without make-up, crown, or garlands, was less regal than on his wedding-night but he looked more human and approachable. He even laughed when I reminded him of the rice-ball episode. His wife clung to his arm possessively. There was no false timidity about her now. She was very conscious of being a 'Madam', in addition to her status of *Raden Aju*, or Princess of Java.

This wedding was the last *kraton* ceremony I attended, but I roamed round the palace gardens many times before I left Jogjakarta, whenever I could disengage myself from my incursions into Javanese magic and mystics which occupied the remainder of my time in this city. I loved everything about the *kraton*: the cambogia blossom, the peacocks, the gamelan pavilion, the graceful deportment of the palace attendants. Above all I loved the easy-going tempo, the inducement to meditation, the cult of beauty and refinement preserved within its walls. The *kraton* is a nucleus of other-worldliness in this brittle Age of the Spanner which is rapidly transforming the old Java into the new. I only hope that the Javanese will continue to revere what the *kraton* stands for and that they will preserve it *ad infinitum*, considering it—and here I quote the delightful expression invented by the artistically sensitive Japanese—as part of Java's 'intangible cultural property'.

PART IV

MAGIC AND MYSTICS OF JAVA

M

A MEDICINE-WOMAN IN THE MARKET-PLACE

IN a Javanese market-place the most ordinary, everyday trans-
actions are sublimated beyond vulgar commercialism—bathed
in human warmth, immersed in exciting odours, staged in
provocative shadows. I have seen a great many market-places
and I lament their decline in England. Our country markets are
not what they used to be. Even Spanish markets are beginning
to be tidied up and pushed into hygienic concrete buildings;
African markets are still jolly and haphazard, but Javanese markets
are in a different category altogether. There is an element of
mystery about them from which even the sophisticated *pasar* of
Jogjakarta beside the bus station was not immune. Probably the
darkness has something to do with this atmosphere and the eerie
tranquillity of the women—for here, as in West Africa, the
womenfolk conduct all the business, except for a few men who
sell ready-made turbans in the front part of the *pasar*.

The cool, controlled voices mingling with the sweet aroma of
tropical fruits and spices drew me back again and again. There
was always so much to look at, linger over, and sample. Although
my 'modern' Javanese friends despised *semolah*, a soft drink of
lemon rind, palm sugar, and nuts that cannot be found elsewhere,
this *pasar* beverage, that only costs ten cents a glass, is infinitely
superior (and certainly healthier) to the synthetic orange-crush of
the more respectable shops. Their disdain is due to the fact that
semolah is not 'modern', it has not been turned out of a factory,
or produced on a conveyer belt, distributed in Western capitals
... it is as homely as grandmother's elderberry wine, and almost
as obsolete.

The cake stall next to the *semolah* stand was a little less appe-
tizing, although the flies appreciated their wares: sticky brown
balls speckled with caraway seeds, slabs of green, white, and pink

173

tapioca cake and behind them half-empty honeycombs visited by wasps. There were enough wide fans of bananas to sicken one of this mealy fruit for life (not even the *pisang mas* can compare in flavour with the bananas from the Canary Islands). Oranges were being sold green, lemons round and unfamiliar, and the yellow, bloated cucumbers were almost unrecognizable. European-introduced vegetables grown high up in the clouds included cabbages, runner beans, and tiny potatoes from the slopes of Mount Merapi. Shelled peanuts, beans—green, red, beige, and black—and rice-grains of all sizes, were piled everywhere with reckless extravagance. I hovered inquiringly over slabs of a creamy substance made from soya beans; some of it was being cut up into thick slices and fried on the spot, but the vendor did not look at me twice—she knew that I was not likely to buy any.

Cheerful mounds of chillies, minute pink onions and *mendiko* that resemble rose-hips and are used for flavouring, tempted me for their colour alone. One side of the *pasar* was reserved for salted fish, dried shrimps, and live creatures—some of them wriggly as eels, others black and moustached, of the same shape as tadpoles. The noisiest section was that set aside for fowls cooped up in round bamboo baskets. Some were tied together in bundles by their feet. The cocks had their eyes bound up with a strip of banana leaf, presumably to keep them from seeing rivals and becoming enraged. Vendors of empty bottles long bereft of corks or stoppers sat hopefully behind their miserable wares which Westerners would have relegated to their dust-heaps. Haughty vendors of *batik* sarongs smoked gravely beside their turban-specialist colleagues, pretending to be a cut above the others. Far behind them in a dark recess ruthless butcher-women on high, bar-like stools hacked sacrificial lumps of fibrous flesh upon marble slabs.

Immediately outside the *pasar* an ambulating youth stopped for a moment to sell fruit juice from large tins suspended from a flexible bamboo yoke which was more ornate than the usual type for not only did it support the tins of juice but, in addition, a mandorla-shaped halo of glasses, ingeniously fitted into bamboo grooves, that sparkled merrily round the vendor's head.

One of the saddest looking vendors in the poultry department was the favourite clown from the town's popular theatre or *Ketoprak*. This in its small way corresponds to the Italian dialect theatre and is to be found tucked away in the humbler districts of Javanese cities. 'It is a very primitive form of entertainment,' said my modern Javanese friends primly, for they are repelled both by the roughness of the language and the clumsiness of the production. *Ketoprak* actors and actresses cannot scrape a living from their precarious profession—and this explained the daytime presence of the clown in the market-place. His nocturnal mimicry of the courtly *Srimpi* dancers made me—as well as the rest of the audience—roar with laughter, particularly his rendering of the ladies' simpering expressions and modest readjustment of a falling sarong. Educated Javanese audiences never clap or manifest any signs of enthusiasm, but the uneducated ones let themselves go to the point of throwing balls of paper on to the stage to show their appreciation. I must admit that I felt very much at ease among them. I enjoyed the slapstick even though I could not follow the involved and probably puerile plots. These are nearly always serials divided into seven instalments to last through the week. Performances begin at nine and end at one o'clock in the morning. They are shorter than the classical *wayang orang* since the performers must rise early to start earning their daily rice and chillies. *Ketoprak* players never have time to rehearse; they are professional improvisers. They sit round their producer about an hour before the show is due to begin when he distributes the roles and gives them a brief exposé of the story to be acted that night. After that it is up to them to work it out for themselves upon the stage. The resulting performance is refreshingly spontaneous although it may not be highly polished.

Nowadays, the manager told me, people prefer detective stories to romances, so he is constantly rummaging about for books which can be adapted to *Ketoprak*. From what I saw of them, these 'adaptations', whatever their origin, are very effectively

Javanized. All kinds of local elements, past and present, are incorporated into the stories: regents, kings of the Madjopahit empire of the Middle Ages, enchanted rings, magic incantations, village doctors, political elections, rifles, bandits, and dwarfs. The *Ketoprak* troupe of Jogjakarta has two fascinating chubby dwarfs attached to it. They appear on the stage in old-style Javanese undress, naked to the waist, brandishing miniature krisses.

Some years ago, the *Ketoprak* manager laid his restless hands on a translation of *Hamlet* which he promptly 'adapted' for his players. He assured me that the audience had greatly appreciated it, particularly the last scene 'which is so effective with all those corpses piled up on the stage,' he remarked. I wondered what Resident John Crawfurd would have thought of this. When he wrote:

'Whatever strangers may think of the dramatic entertainments of the Javanese, they excite a deep and lively interest in a native audience. The habit of listening to such performances convinces me that it would be no difficult matter to introduce among them a more improved drama. In the first instance such performances might be adapted to their tastes by being built on the foundation of their own legends. A judicious paraphrase of *The Tempest*, for example, composed on this principle I have little doubt would be eminently successful. The effects of such exhibitions as an instrument of civilization need not be insisted upon . . .'

I am afraid Crawfurd did not realize what *Ketoprak* could do to Shakespeare!

The most taciturn of all the people in the market-place is the medicine-woman. She squats in a dark corner, pounding a weird concoction of herbs in a small bowl, her lips brick-red from constant chewing of betel-nuts and lime paste which she sells to other withered crones as a sideline. She is frequently engaged in making up preparations to keep women slim after child-bearing. Most Javanese women drink all kinds of plant mixtures for this and other purposes. Whether it is because of them or because of the way in which they are built, Javanese women certainly succeed in keeping amazingly slim even after they have had as many as ten or twelve children.

The old witch doctor or *dukun* is said to be very powerful and to be able to exorcise people to whom poison has been administered surreptitiously by other less efficient magicians. A Western-trained Javanese doctor told me the following curious story about her:

A year ago, a patient was admitted to the general hospital with a swollen leg which was causing him acute pain. He had a very high temperature and was almost delirious. The doctor examined him thoroughly but could not discover the cause of his illness. He tried all sorts of remedies, but nothing would reduce the swelling or the man's discomfort and in the end he had to confess that he was quite baffled.

This man had not wanted to go to the hospital himself—his family had insisted upon his admittance. Three days later, as the doctor was standing at the foot of his bed, wondering what to do next, the man beckoned him to draw close as there was something he wanted to confide in him. When the doctor bent over him he whispered hoarsely: 'Doctor, you may be very clever, but my trouble is of a nature that no ordinary doctor can cure. I implore you, if you really want to help me, send for the *dukun* of my village.' Another doctor would probably have pooh-poohed such a fantastic, unscientific notion but although my friend had been trained in the West he had never lost contact with his people and their ways and he does not believe that all native medical lore is pure charlatanism; so, to the astonishment of his staff, he sent for the village *dukun*, who turned out to be a woman—the old woman of the market-place. She came to the hospital at once; she had been expecting to be called, she said. The doctor watched her closely as she went up to the sick man and passed her hands lightly over his leg; even this light touch seemed to cause him unbearable pain. Then she stopped, closed her eyes, and mumbled something to herself, swaying from side to side like a person in a trance.

After two or three minutes she straightened herself up, opened her eyes, and looked at the ward nurse who was eyeing her with an air of disdainful scepticism. 'Bring me an egg—a fresh egg,' demanded the *dukun*. The ward nurse stiffened and was about to refuse point-blank when the doctor intervened. 'Do as she says— bring her an egg,' he ordered. The nurse obeyed with great reluctance. While she was fetching the egg, the *dukun* spoke to the patient in low, encouraging tones; he listened to her attentively and with a respect which he had never shown to the doctor!

When the nurse returned with the egg, the *dukun* took it from her and clasped it in her hands, which she held close to her mouth while she breathed over it, muttering some inaudible incantation. Then she pulled down the sheet and proceeded to roll the egg over the patient's leg. He screamed in agony but the *dukun* only pursed her lips and continued to roll the egg up and down. This went on for about two minutes at the end of which she looked up at the nurse and asked her to bring a bowl. Upon a sign from the doctor, the exasperated nurse brought her what she wanted. The *dukun* held the egg close to her ear, shook it, nodded with satisfaction and then, with a sudden brisk gesture, she broke the egg against the side of the bowl and poured the contents inside.

The onlookers gasped, and the nurse paled visibly as she bent forward to look. For there in the centre of the bowl were—they counted them carefully afterwards—*two dozen needles!* The *dukun* smiled grimly. 'That's why he was in such pain,' she said simply. 'His enemy in the village wished him harm and had a spell cast over him, but the *dukun* he went to is not as powerful as I am!' The doctor forgave her for looking so jubilant. He said he would have been proud of such success himself. Was it a mere conjuring trick? Whatever it was, the swelling subsided almost immediately and the man was discharged from hospital the very next day.

BLACK MAGIC

FROM amulets to satanic invocations, from village *dukuns* to secret societies, the whole magic armoury of the groping universe is well known and frequently used by the spirit-conscious Javanese. 'What is thy name?' Christ asked the spirit that possessed the man from the tombs in the cemetery of the Gadarenes, and it replied: 'My name is Legion.' A large portion of this legion appears to have emigrated to Java where its members have met with considerable success and from what I saw and heard they are not likely to be deposed from their exalted position in the near future.

I once asked a Javanese who was familiar with various categories of spirits whether he would be kind enough to list them for me, but he evaded the issue by exclaiming that they were far too numerous and that he could not remember all their names. Nevertheless, he mentioned quite a few. First of all, the devils, or 'satans', who include: *tetekans*, *janggitans*, *banaspatis*, and *ilu-ilu*. These are beings of the lowest order. Above them, and less malevolent, are the musical *ghandarvas* (from India), the *weiwees*, *peris* (from Persia), *pragangans*, and djinns (these do not have to be italicized; we know them well from the *Arabian Nights*). Then there are the beneficent *devas* or angels of God and the archangels Gabriel and Michael who are always in communication with mankind. Gabriel is said to be in close contact with the Almighty. (He used to be frequently invoked by English astrologers.) The angel who went astray—our Lucifer—is called *Idyadril*. It would appear, from this international pantheon of spirits and angels, that a few of them are common to East and West. Javanese poltergeists too, from what I was told, behave in very much the same way as they do in Great Britain. The Javanese are extremely interested in the fey world and quite prepared to welcome fresh arrivals, even from Western shores. Their eyes glistened when I spoke to them about Cornish pixies, Irish fairies, elves, and goblins. They had never heard of these little folk before, but their hearts warmed to them at once. Could I not persuade some of them to come to Java? I promised that I would put the proposition to them upon my return, through people who are on closer terms with them than I—such as those who write testimonials to pixies in our popular almanacks. But to return to the indigenous spirits and beliefs of Java:

Several important *batik* manufacturers of Jogjakarta keep spirits called *tujluns* in their house who help them to prosper in their business in return for certain sacrifices, preferably human. This does not imply that the *batik* manufacturers hold periodical holocausts of elements selected from their ageing or least efficient workers—such a practice would hardly be conducive to the development of the industry. No, the pact is carried out more subtly than that. The *tujlun* itself brings about the apparently natural death of the workers marked for it in the factory by the provision of special food. It is not excessively greedy and does not take a toll of more than one or two craftsmen per year, so that no suspicions are aroused.

Petty thieves are notorious dabblers in black magic. I have already mentioned how careful they are to plan their *coups* after a detailed study of the auspicious days in the Javanese calendar. In addition, some of them cultivate occult gifts to assist them in their nefarious enterprises. For example, they procure soil from a fresh grave in the nearest cemetery and throw it over the house they intend to burgle, causing the inmates to fall into a deep, trance-like sleep. (This is less lugubrious than certain magic practices of West Africa in which pieces of the actual corpse are disinterred for similar purposes.)

Many are the devices resorted to by *dukuns* in order to improve their clients' appeal to the opposite sex. A diamond blown on to the lips by a *dukun* will give his customer a perfectly irresistible smile and fascination for the fair sex; a gold needle inserted into the middle of his forehead produces similar results a little more painfully. In the West, we drink soluble iron in the form of tonics to strengthen us, but the *dukuns* believe it is more effective to push pieces of iron up your arm; iron is also attached to footballers' legs to give added force to their limbs. What with this and their years of limbering up with *penchak* exercises, Indonesian footballers can be doughty opponents.

Spirits can possess human beings physically and shower riches and worldly blessings upon them in exchange for sexual favours. I knew that the Shamans of Central India are alleged to 'marry' spirits and have many children by them in the underworld, but I was surprised to learn from a 'usually reliable source' that certain high-bred Javanese families in and around Jogjakarta have put aside a special room in their house for their sexual relations with a spirit that assumes human form for this purpose. The son of a distinguished lady told my informant that his mother never allows anybody—not even the servants—to enter this unholy sanctuary in her house.

Of another nature altogether are the spirits embodied for life in ceremonial krisses, especially those forged for rulers and noblemen. The *kraton* possesses some exquisite examples of these. The men who forged them with steel and that stone from heaven beloved by sorcerers all over the world, the meteorite, breathed incantations over their furnaces and blew spirits of their own creation into the blades to dwell in them for ever. Some of these spirits are evil and destructive while others on the contrary are helpful and protective. A cultured and scientifically trained Javanese gentleman of great charm, whom I met in Solo, has the gift of social intercourse with the spirits of krisses. He is well known for this strange faculty and krisses have been brought to him from all over Java, either for 'analysis' or as presents, for he attracts krisses unto himself as others attract love or riches. He showed me some of his choice specimens: sixteenth-century krisses in finely wrought gold sheaths with curved polished handles of rare tropical woods shaped like inverted tomahawks, given to him by the princes of the court. One of the krisses now hangs in the front porch of his house since its spirit, which appeared to him in the form of a young boy, entreated to be allowed to remain out of doors, where he would protect the house from danger. Another powerful spirit had elected to join this gentleman's collection of its own accord and had implored its previous owner to carry it to him, which he did. A superb seventeenth-century kris —also brought as a present—was eventually returned to its original owner, for its spirit was discovered to be a jealousy-inspiring demon who sowed domestic discord wherever it went!

Cave spirits and crossroad spirits, river and tree spirits—all of these abound in Java. A Western-educated Javanese who works at the Health Ministry of a large city, told me the following story —a true story, he assured me—about his uncle's negotiations with a tree spirit.

A peasant in a nearby village wanted to sell a plot of land but he could not get rid of it at any price because of a large banyan tree in the centre which was said to be inhabited by a harmful spirit. This spirit refused to allow anyone to cultivate the land round the tree and had the unpleasant habit of casting curses upon anybody who tried to do so.

My friend's uncle came to hear about this and he decided to go and buy the land himself because—explained my friend—he had the gift of being able to converse with tree spirits. The owner of the land was delighted to find a buyer and he parted with it for next to nothing for he was only too glad to be relieved of this burden. As soon as he was in possession, my friend's uncle walked up to the banyan tree and, addressing the spirit who lived there, tried to persuade it to move somewhere else. 'How would you like to live beside the stream that flows at the foot of Mount Merapi?' he suggested. 'It is a lovely spot and it would make a change for you.' 'Well,' answered the spirit after a little thought, 'as a matter of fact, I could do with a change. I am getting a little weary of this tree and besides it's rather lonely. People are so afraid of me that they won't come near the place, just because I amused myself by teasing them a little when I first came here. They have told awful lies about the things I did to them. How you human beings love to exaggerate! But *you* don't believe them, do you? I can see that you are a reasonable sort of man and understanding. Very well, then, I agree to your proposition, on condition you carry me down to the stream on your back and give a really good *slametan* in my honour when we get there. On second thoughts,' added the spirit, 'I should like you to give a *slametan* in my name every year; in exchange, I promise never to come back to this tree any more.' 'Well,' said my friend very seriously, 'my uncle agreed to the spirit's conditions and he carried it on his back all the way to the stream and then offered a *slametan*, and everything has gone well with him ever since. He has cultivated the land round the banyan tree and made a handsome profit out of it.'

THE MAN WHO SAW MY SEVEN LIVES

THE bald, apish little man in front of me grinned behind his spectacles as he sat dangling his short legs on a chair in the Prince's office. I had been warned that he was one of Jogjakarta's 'characters', a minor civil servant and—in his leisure hours—an independent mystic and grand dabbler in occultism. His particular gift in this line lay in his capacity to conjure up people's past lives. I have met Europeans who possess this peculiar gift too, which they often exercise through the medium of psychometry; that is, they 'see' past lives after having captured the vibrations given off by a ring or other personal object frequently worn by the subject. But Mr. H.'s method was quite different and infinitely more entertaining. *He* did not need to finger any object beforehand. One sharp look at his subject sets him off immediately on a series of seven visions, never more, never less, which he proceeds to mimic with the histrionic ability of a *Ketoprak* clown. Each of these seven acts represents the species of animal or the kind of person incarnated by the subject during his previous lives.

Mr. H. has been ostracized by the members of the mystic circle to which he formerly belonged, because he is said to be a bit of an anarchist in the visionary sphere, who refuses to abide by the circle's rules. The leader of this mystic circle, which I shall describe more fully in the next chapter, does not approve of his disciples showing off their occult gifts. Nor does he think that it is particularly useful for anybody to know what he or she was in the course of previous existences. The accumulation of experience gained in them (which the Indians call *sanskara*) has to be worked out in our present existence under the guidance of the spiritual beacon which lightens our individual paths: Christ for the Christians, Mohammed for the Muslims, and so on.

Mr. H. was the very personification of a quack—an amiable, wizened quack with a Rabelaisian sense of humour. The Prince had invited him on my behalf by way of an occult *divertissement*, and he continued to look tolerantly amused throughout the novel performance. I afterwards regretted that I had not taken my cine-camera with me. Just imagine the effect of observing casually to one's friends at a cocktail party: 'Oh, by the way, would you like to see the film of my seven lives?' No hostess in London could have matched that. I would have been unique. And what splendid material for the gossip columnists whom I would have invited to the party!

Not that there is anything of a very flattering nature about these seven lives of mine as seen by Mr. H., who has no ideas of grandeur and is no respecter of persons. It was, however, refreshing to learn that I had *not* been the Queen of Sheba, Joan of Arc, Mrs. Siddons, or somebody equally notorious. An elderly lady in Paris once informed me that I had been a seal in my animal existence. This was a pleasant thought, for I have a deep affection for seals, but so have a great many other people and I do not suppose that we were all seals together once upon a time. The seal, however, is a northern creature; Mr. H. had probably never heard of it, and he could not impersonate the unknown. All he saw was of a tropical nature . . . the obvious outcome of his environment or memories of his readings and visits to the cinema, just as the most genuine mystics in their trances see symbols associated with their own personal experiences and beliefs.

'Well,' said the Prince inquiringly, 'shall we begin?' Mr. H. nodded brightly, jumped off his chair (I wondered what *he* had been in his animal existence) and stood for a few seconds in the middle of the room, looking out of the window in the direction of Mecca—although Mecca would have rejected such unorthodoxy outright. He was presumably concentrating. Then he fell forward with acrobatic agility and began to crawl upon all fours, snorting and grimacing. We were asked to call out the name of whatever creature we thought he was impersonating. 'A whale', I suggested; this was evidently incorrect for Mr. H. shook his head and proceeded with his antics. 'A walrus?' I ventured again. Still wrong. 'A sea lion?' No. Finally, he had to tell us himself. He had seen me as a hippopotamus disporting myself in the waters of the Nile some few thousand years ago. Once again he stood and concentrated in the direction of Mecca before lurching forward and leaping madly round the room with a distorted facial expression. There was no doubt about this one. 'A monkey!' I declared, correctly. After this life I apparently passed into the human kingdom, but with a pronounced limp. (What could I have done wrong in my monkey state to deserve this affliction?) Mr. H. stumped about for some time, but neither the prince nor I could think who I was supposed to be. 'An American historian,' Mr. H. was obliged to inform us. Then he looked at me a little doubtfully. 'Or it might have been Tom Mix,' he added.

The next one was easy. 'A beggar!' I exclaimed as Mr. H. began to crawl round obsequiously with uplifted hands and a doleful face. Yes, a beggar in Djakarta. (No wonder I have such a deep-rooted loathing for this city!) The fifth life was socially and mentally superior. Mr. H. drew himself up to his full height with an arrogant mien, made sweeping gestures with an imaginary cloak and stretched his hand in blessing. I was a famous 'Roman' (he meant Italian) religious leader and preacher. During my sixth life I was back in Java as a *penchak* teacher in the area of Bandung. This life does not appear to have left any noticeable mark upon me. I have never felt the urge to take up jiu-jitsu or *penchak*—although I have felt the urge to return to Java! After a final concentration, Mr. H. spun round and fell at my feet with a smile. This meant that I was enjoying my seventh life at that moment. I was 'myself'. He concluded by making a brief analysis of my character, which included a few forthright home truths. Mr. H. is certainly very frank for a Central Javanese. Later on, he 'acted' the Prince's lives. I should love to be able to tell you about them, but the Prince made me cross my heart and promise never to reveal such intimate secrets.

Mr. H. stayed for lunch and entertained us—when the servants were out of earshot—with extraordinary tales about the re-incarnation of souls. He told us, for instance, how he had dis-covered that a gardener's dog—which was particularly attached to its master—had been his father in a previous life. On another occasion, two of his friends were praying for their father's soul; he had died some years before and since they were both visionaries they could see his soul pacing to and fro, anxious to be re-incarnated. At that time the wife of one of the brothers hap-pened to be pregnant. 'Shall I make father's soul enter your wife's womb?' suggested the other brother jocularly. 'Wouldn't it be amusing to have father back again as your son?' I have already referred to the fact that some Javanese are not lacking in a medieval sense of humour.

It is obvious from the above story that certain Javanese seers are convinced they have the power to direct a soul to its destina-tion, either when it is on its way back to a body upon the earth, or when it is ascending heavenwards after death.

Mr. H. told us that when his own wife—also a visionary—was dying, she could see her soul struggling skywards and she kept on asking him weakly, as her earthly sight diminished: 'Is this where my soul is to rest?' as it flitted from mansion to mansion in distant spheres. 'No,' he whispered, 'not yet—go on—farther —farther. . . .' 'Is this it now?' she asked again a little later. 'Still farther—higher. . . .' 'And now?' 'Yes, there you are— that is where you must rest.' And at that instant she died. Is there not an astonishing similarity between this story and the splendid scene in *Pier Gynt*, when rollicking Pier eases his old mother's death by pretending to escort her to the gates of heaven on his sleigh?

LORO KIDUL, GODDESS OF THE SOUTH SEA

ALTHOUGH the Javanese, being Muslims, are supposed to believe in one God, many of them are inclined to fall back into their old Hindu polytheistic trends of thought and to pay homage to lesser divinities. The most popular of these is the Goddess Loro Kidul, who is said to live in the Indian Ocean on Java's south coast and who protects the Sultan's palace in Jogjakarta. She is rather like a Queen Neptune, with a court of attractive sea-nymphs and other not so attractive guards whose green hair is encrusted with shells, limpets, and seaweed. At least, so I have been told by Javanese mystics who assured me that they have seen these strange creatures with their own eyes.

They have also seen Loro Kidul appear (out of sheer curiosity, they assured me) during the collective meditations of their mystic fraternity. She would like to become a member of this fraternity herself, they say—but, fearing her wiles and occult powers, their leader has firmly refused to sponsor her admittance. He believes that she is the incarnation of a famous Sultan who practised black magic during his lifetime.

Loro Kidul was frequently invoked by the Emperors of Solo, who had a special tower built in their *kraton* for their rendezvous with her. Since this tower was burned down the fickle lady is alleged to have transferred her affections to the *kraton* of Jogjakarta, where she used to take afternoon tea with the Sultan who built the Water Palace. In those days tea used to be served in style by the Sultan's Grand Pourer Out on the Right and his Grand Pourer Out on the Left. These imposing but not very useful functionaries have long ceased to exist. (Western imperialism dealt cruelly with the grandiloquent titles that used to be taken so seriously in Asia before we appeared on the scene.)

Loro Kidul's noisy bodyguard of nymphs beating percussion

188

instruments liked to swim upstream through Jogjakarta and beyond this city to Mount Merapi, with whom the goddess occasionally conversed, but the inhabitants have not heard this army, called 'Lampor', for a long time. Perhaps that is because they do not listen for it as fearfully as they used to.

Not only does the Goddess Loro Kidul receive offerings from the faithful gathered on the southern shores every Thursday—on the eve of the Muslim's day of rest—and an extra special offering once a year on behalf of the Sultan, but also an 'opening of the season' ceremony in her honour before the springtime collection of edible swallows' nests. These nests built in the crevices of the rocks along the coast are eaten by the Chinese who live in Java, but the dangerous task of collecting them from the steep cliff face is undertaken by the Javanese peasants who live near the shore.

Not a single nest is touched, however, before the Goddess Loro Kidul is invoked by a Javanese gamelan orchestra. The musicians sit cross-legged on the beach and first beat their gongs to inform the goddess that the ceremony is about to begin. Most of the men who play in the gamelan will climb up to collect the swallows' nests when the ritual is over. But before doing so their womenfolk carry food offerings to the edge of the sea for the goddess and her court of nymphs. They bring rice, bananas, and coconuts placed upon flat bamboo trays prettily decorated with forest flowers and streamers made from palm leaves. In addition, two of the elder women carry a large wooden carving of a bird that looks very much like an eagle. This is Garuda, the mythological bird of the Hindu epics. On this particular occasion, he is set down on the sands for Loro Kidul to use as a carrier between the waves and the shore. Next a mirror and a tray full of makeup articles is placed beside the Garuda bird so that the goddess, who is eternally young and therefore concerned with her personal appearance, can tidy herself up when she steps down from Garuda's back after the long journey from her palace beneath the sea. A comb, face powder, carbon black for her eyes, betel leaves for her lips and perfume, are thoughtfully laid out at the foot of the mirror, and bowls of incense and flower petals are set round it to indicate that these offerings are intended for a divine being.

In the meantime, the men implore the goddess to protect them during their hazardous mission and to give them a plentiful harvest of birds' nests. Very soon one of the players half-closes his eyes and passes into a trance. The Javanese have the knack of being able to attain this state far more rapidly than the average European. In his trance-state the player begins to have visions and to describe them in a high-pitched nasal voice. He sees the Goddess Loro Kidul, he says . . . 'she is riding over the foam-crested waves—she has answered their call; soon she will shake off the shoals of fish and shells that cling to her gold-embroidered sarong and her raven hair, and step upon the shore' . . .

The playing subsides as the men close their eyes in meditation to be able to share the vision. Thanks to the most sensitive trance-medium among them, all of them can now see the graceful form of Loro Kidul who, after having combed her long tresses and admired her reflection in the mirror, advances to greet them and to imbue them with supernatural strength and agility. This is the most awesome moment of the ceremony and all is silent save for the lapping of the waves upon the sandy shore.

Sometimes the vision of the goddess only lasts for a few seconds; at other times it may last a little longer, appearing and then vanishing with the suddenness of a rainbow. When it is over, one of the men exclaims: '*Sampun!*' (It is finished.) Then they shake themselves, lay aside their instruments, and walk over to the cliffs to begin their tricky climb, barefoot, on narrow bamboo ladders and along an alarmingly elastic bamboo scaffolding that leads into the caves where the nests are to be found. But the men are as confident and casual as our window cleaners and steeplejacks. They are used to dizzy heights and narrow ledges and, above all, their vision of Loro Kidul has assured them of the success of their undertaking. Nobody will fall, there will be no accidents. Loro Kidul, who commands the whole of this coast, will see to that.

When I walked to Parangtritis, the nearest beach from Jogjakarta, the little boy who darted out from one of the many bamboo

restaurant-shacks along the sands entreated me to buy two coconuts from him—one for myself, and one to throw into the waves
for Loro Kidul. At first I mistook him for a diminutive commercial cynic, but after some conversation (he attached himself to
me for the rest of the day), I realized that he was quite sincere.
He was eight years old, full of urchin charm, and a *lolo*, he told
me sadly. This pathetic little word is Indonesian for 'orphan',
and it can sound very mournful when it is pronounced by a thin-
faced little boy with large, appealing black eyes. The *lolo* was a
chainsmoker of *kreteks*; he had given up going to school and was
living for the day when he could become a *betjak* boy in Jogjakarta. The great white bars of the Indian Ocean roared in front
of us like enraged lions. I looked in vain for fishing-craft. 'Don't
people fish round here?' I asked. The *lolo* shook his head and
pointed gravely to the surf. 'Loro Kidul doesn't like it,' he said
simply.

INTRODUCTION TO SUMARAH:
CLIMBING A SPIRITUAL EVEREST

THE Javanese, who are as interested in spirits as our north country folk are in ghosts and who take the supernatural as a matter of course like the rising and setting of the sun, are equally attracted by mysticism—or communion with the infinite—with a view to their spiritual training and development.

Their spiritual urge is so intense that new religious sects are constantly being devised and officially registered by the Ministry of Religious Affairs, while unorthodox mystic societies flourish to such an extent that a 'Congress of Mystic Groups' had recently been convened in North Java.

Even Western incursions into these spheres are gratefully accepted and followed alongside other amiable heresies. I met several people in Jogjakarta who were not only members of a Javanese mystic fraternity but who also belonged to the local branch of the Theosophical Society, in spite of the wide breach between the tenets of the two.

Is there, as has often been maintained, more of a religious climate in the East than in the West? I would say that possibly there is but that it is due to the time lag in historical development between the two. The East today is as religiously conscious as we were, say, in the seventeenth century when most Europeans held strong, even fanatical beliefs, and superstitions were as current among the non-educated classes as they are in Java at the present time.

The Javanese rarely discuss these subjects with Westerners, for they believe that we are of a too grossly materialistic turn of mind. Since they were colonized by the not very metaphysical Dutch and are almost totally ignorant of Christian mystics, they shut themselves up like sea-anemones in our presence, afraid of being despised as 'backward, superstitious natives'. They therefore expressed astonishment when I announced that I was interested in mysticism and asked whether somebody could tell me about its influence and following in Java. My friends in Djakarta, who are superficially more Westernized than those of Jogjakarta, have made up their minds that it is neither 'modern' nor practicable to be mystical and so they could give me no help; many of them suffer from a split personality and feel that if they were to follow their natural Javanese bent and go off into mystical trances, they would never catch up with the Age of the Spanner and the Atom at all, so they have resolutely turned away from such temptations, confusing mysticism—as so many people do here as elsewhere—with all that is irrational and of a woolly nature. They would do well to ponder over what the contemporary Indian mystic Meher Baba has to say in this connection:

'Mysticism', he has explained to his followers, 'is unclouded perception, and so practical that it can be lived every moment of life and expressed in everyday duties; its connection with experience is so deep that it is the final understanding of all experience. If the soul loses its connection with experience and the different phases of life, there is a neurotic reaction, which is far from being a spiritual experience—for this not only involves the realization of the soul on higher planes, but a right attitude to worldly duties and everyday life.' There is nothing airy-fairy or escapist about this.

Many esoteric groups and fraternities of Java are merely a cover for the development and practice of occult powers and black magic. But my friends in Jogjakarta assured me—as if we had been discussing banks or insurance companies—that one society, called 'Sumarah', was: 'the most reliable mystical fraternity' in Java, meaning thereby that their objectives were lofty and came under the category of 'white magic'. They arranged for me to meet the Secretary of the Jogjakarta branch, Mr. Sardjono, who was employed in the local Health Ministry. Fortunately both Mr. Sardjono and his wife spoke English well, for during the next few weeks they found themselves called upon to do an enormous amount of interpreting and difficult translating of the sometimes obscure incantations of their leader, Mr. Sukino, the Javanese bank clerk who founded Sumarah in 1937. This fraternity has now seven thousand members enrolled in thirty-four branches throughout Indonesia, and it is greatly respected.

Sumarah is not a secret society, but I happen to be one of the few Europeans who have had the opportunity of attending their meetings. I shall now attempt to describe some of these, from an external point of view. To attempt to explain the inner, spiritual effects of Sumarah would need another book. But even a detailed book is unsatisfactory as a means of communicating intangibles. Language—whether spoken or written—is limited to the conscious world of the five senses, and spiritual exercises through meditation as practised in Sumarah sessions must actually be experienced under guidance. One cannot fully understand them through merely verbal accounts.

Neither physical exercises such as Yoga nor asceticism are used as a means to spiritual unfolding; the aspirant pledges himself to fulfil the Sumarah 'vows' (see Appendix), after which he joins the beginners' class, or A grade of the seven degrees initiation. The seventh degree initiates are in the visionary class but they do not publicize their visions. This would be contrary to the spirit of humility and self-surrender to God which is the core of Sumarah doctrine.

Sumarah is in many ways so characteristic both of the Eastern mind and of the universal yearning after the infinite that I intend to devote the remaining pages of this book to a summary account of its activities. What follows is a glimpse of the 'inner' Java, unmasked and unveiled, as her own people—but few outsiders—know her.

FOR LADIES ONLY

TWICE a week, the lady members of Sumarah meet in a humble house at the edge of Jogjakarta for their collective meditation classes. Mrs. Sardjono, who was preparing for her first-grade initiation, escorted me there in a *betjak*; her husband followed us in a second *betjak* for in his capacity of secretary he was allowed to penetrate into the 'ladies only' group, in order to answer my many questions.

The *betjak* stopped us before a door in a high wall opposite a grove of coconut palms. At the far end of the road, I caught a brief glimpse of green paddy-fields and the bluish blur of Mount Merapi, its summit mantled in cloud. The door opened on to a little compound of bungalows separated by neatly swept paths and gardens in which orchid plants were suspended from boards of some fibrous substance, like chemical specimens in a laboratory. A few chubby children were playing among the ducks. Mrs. Sardjono stepped daintily between the bungalows; at the end of the compound she paused before an open door and began to remove her shoes. I followed her example, observing from the many sandals strewn around that we had been preceded by quite a number of ladies.

Mrs. Sardjono pushed the door gently open, bowing low as she did so and falling on her heels in the Javanese *dodok* posture which is not considered servile in Jogjakarta—as it is in Djakarta—but simply a mark of courtesy among equals. The open door revealed a narrow room, empty of furniture, spread with fresh woven grass mats that replace our carpet, tables and chairs. A sewing-machine in a corner indicated that the room belonged to a woman —who sat at the opposite end squatting in the centre of about twenty little ladies in sarongs. While they waited for the rest of the class to arrive, they engaged in soft, dove-like conversation, with their feet crossed and their hands meekly folded in their laps. The leader of the ladies' groups, grey-haired Mrs. Sujitno, is a widow who earns her living as a highly skilled *batik* worker, in her own home. She is also the secretary of the local Theosophical Society. The only European language she knew was of course Dutch, which she spoke fluently. Lively, smiling, efficient Mrs. Sujitno commanded her group with gentle authority. A few days later, however, I saw her handle the gavel at a masculine meeting with somewhat more severity. I have met prioresses of convents who combine the same complementary qualities: a keen sense of organization and considerable spiritual ascendancy.

The group had been forewarned that a European woman was coming to assist at their class and they welcomed me with friendly smiles that soon turned to good-natured laughter when I endeavoured to creep up the room in the formal *dodok* posture. '*Monggo!*' they murmured in salutation as Mrs. Sardjono and I finally reached Mrs. Sujitno's side. She raised merry brown eyes to mine as I squatted inelegantly beside her. Mr. Sardjono joined us noiselessly and began to whisper a running commentary on the proceedings for my benefit.

There were two small rooms leading off the one in which we had assembled so that the three groups of ladies, who were at different stages of spiritual development could separate for their meditations. A first or grade A initiation ceremony was about to take place and the grade A guide was pointed out to me: she was a wrinkled, illiterate old lady dressed in a modest sarong. Illiteracy, far from being a handicap, is sometimes an aid to spiritual progress, explained Mr. Sardjono; the trouble with the more educated aspirants is that they have usually read too much and their brains are full of confused and conflicting theories. They find it particularly difficult to 'empty their minds of thought' which is the prerequisite of abstract meditation and concentration. Intellectuals do not find it easy to 'by-pass' their active brain in order to reach the formless spheres of mystical communication.

The women gathered there in the dim bamboo twilight came

196

from all walks of life. Two of the elder ones had brought their servants and I was told that the latter were spiritually farther advanced than their mistress—a fact accepted with humility on both sides. This spiritual democracy was taken as a matter of course, but I found it profoundly moving. I presume that many readers will now be asking themselves the very question which I then put to Mr. Sardjono: 'Who determines the stage of spiritual enlightenment reached by individual aspirants?' Apparently, periodical checks are made during the collective meditations of the higher-grade groups under their respective leaders. Whenever there is any doubt the subject is referred to yet another group and in the last resort—but this is a rare occurrence—to the Sumarah founder and *guru*, Mr. Sukino. Since the spiritual path is beset with the dangers of self-deception and the temptations of satanic pride, it is often necessary to curb aspirants' flights of fancy which are even capable of affecting their reason. Later on, I saw one of these 'collective verifications' for myself at a meeting presided over by Mr. Sukino.

*   *   *   *

The gentle feminine chatter ceased suddenly upon a sign from the regal Mrs. Sujitno and the shining black heads bent forward to empty their minds of mundane thoughts as a prelude to their meditations. I looked down at the avenue of faces become grave and infinitely serene. All traces of care seemed to have been miraculously removed and they looked as peaceful as the Dhyani-Buddhas of the Borobodur.

After a few minutes of this quiet preparation, the little ladies shuffled themselves like a pack of cards and divided into three groups; two of these flowed into the small rooms, led by their 'guides'. Mr. Sardjono beckoned and I slipped in after him and Mrs. Sardjono to watch the first-grade initiation of two young women. Simplicity and sincerity were the keynotes of the ceremony. The candidates stood facing the west, where Mecca lies. It was explained to me that this position is not essential—it is merely a concession 'to avoid offending the Muslims', for Sumarah, alone among Javanese mystic societies, is tolerant enough to acknowledge the major prophets and to accept aspirants of all creeds. Since, however, the majority of the aspirants are in fact Muslims, the Arabic word for God, Allah, and whole sentences from the Koran, are used during the invocations, but Christians may substitute whichever words they prefer.

The guide took up her position behind the candidates and began to chant the rhythmical 'Allah' in a low, singing voice. There is no doubt that this word is better suited to incantatory purposes than our short, monosyllabic word 'God'. In the meanwhile the candidates were supposed to be directing their consciousness to a central point in their breast with the object of 'neutralizing' their mind so as to bring about an awakening of their static, slumbering soul, through Divine Grace.

The aged and illiterate guide was perfectly aware of what was going on in her aspirants' minds and hearts. A few weeks later when she 'initiated' a Christian, she told Mrs. Sujitno that the aspirant's soul had already been 'awakened' and that no first-degree initiation was necessary in her case. Asked to explain the possible cause of this unusual phenomenon, the aspirant said that in her opinion the sacrament of Holy Communion in her faith must have the same quickening spiritual effect.

It is this *longing* for unison with the infinite which singles out mystic aspirants in the Eastern as well as in the Western hemispheres; the longing that nothing earthly can ever satisfy. 'You will begin to feel different from now on, provided you persevere,' murmured the old guide to the aspirants after they had prayed for nearly ten minutes together. 'There will be a new happiness in your life—always—if you keep to your Sumarah vows.' In her own way, she was defining that state described at length—among others—by our English contemporary C. S. Lewis in his book *Surprised by Joy*.

The grade A initiates are enjoined to practise their meditation exercises at home either sitting or lying down but never standing, as they do during the collective meditations under a guide, for it is said that this position favours the assault of the newly-quickened soul by the forces of evil. Such diabolical manifestations have been experienced by numerous Western mystics, particularly by those in an advanced stage. To take only one curious example from Christian annals: it is recorded of the fifteenth-century Italian mystic Eustochium of Padua that 'the evil spirit who possessed her, controlling her lips, made her tell her Confessor in the presence of other nuns that she was guilty of the crimes imputed to her, such as having conspired to murder the Abbess by poison or enchantment', etc.

The object of the first-grade initiation exercises is to subjugate desires or, as the Javanese call them, the *nafsus*—especially those of greed, anger, and pride. Once these persistent *nafsus* have been quelled (alas, there is always the possibility that they will rear their ugly heads again; few are those who have freed themselves permanently from their insidious tentacles!) the novice is ready to enter the B or second-grade initiation. It is usual in this case for a number of aspirants to be initiated together.

The keyword of all Sumarah meditations, from the first to the seventh grade, is '*sujud*', i.e. submission—submission to the will of God; during the collective exercises, guides are often heard to repeat: '*Sujud, sujud*' in order to focus a wandering mind upon the purpose of the exercise. Christians used to repeating the phrases in the Lord's Prayer: 'Thy will be done', find that *sujud* merely heightens its significance.

THE SECOND SUMARAH INITIATION, AND AFTER

SOME days later, Mr. Sardjono sent a message over asking me whether I would like to assist at a second-degree initiation ceremony that was to take place one evening that week in a kampong some twelve miles north of Jogjakarta. I was delighted to have this opportunity and it was subsequently arranged that I should go in a car belonging to one of the more affluent Sumarah members.

We set off on a wet, dark night with the tropical rain pouring down upon the roof of the car like steel rods. The faithful Mr. Sardjono accompanied us. Would the leader of Sumarah, Mr. Sukino, be there, I wondered, but Mr. Sardjono shook his head with a faint smile. I would meet him later, he promised, at one of the advanced classes which are held more infrequently than those for beginners on the spiritual plane, who are in need of extra guidance and guardianship until they are better able to 'walk by themselves'.

The car slowed up eventually in front of a dimly-lit bamboo house by the side of the main road; a row of ghostly figures were standing as erect as caryatids in the porch, silently waiting for our arrival. They darted forward with umbrellas as soon as they saw us and then led us into a humbly furnished interior where we were introduced to about two dozen rather formal-looking gentlemen—some were Sumarah members and others were village authorities to whom Sumarah was yet unknown. It had been deemed wise to invite them lest they suspected the fraternity of harbouring political intentions. Sumarah is of a mystic but not a mysterious nature and—unlike many self-centred, esoteric groups of 'intellectual' cranks in the West—its leaders have no wish to shroud their aims and practices in puerile veils of secrecy.

There was no electricity in the kampong and coconut-oil lamps cast tremulous patterns upon the walls and faces of all those present; we sat stiffly in rattan armchairs while bowing youths glided towards us from a recess at the back to pour out glasses of tea and present us with palm-sugared cakes. A low murmur rose and fell in the room behind us where the initiates were preparing themselves for the ceremony. The guide who was to initiate them had come from Jogjakarta. It was his first visit to this kampong and he did not know any of the candidates. It was therefore all the more remarkable that he should later address them individually in the course of the ceremony, pointing out the pitfalls to which their different temperaments rendered them particularly vulnerable.

After tea came the inevitable speeches of welcome by our host and a prominent Sumarah member, and a brief explanation of the meaning of Sumarah intended for the village authorities, who listened attentively throughout with polite and slightly awed interest. They seemed to be slightly perplexed by the presence of a Westerner. This was also explained to them at some length.

The 'initiation room' at the back was in near darkness, bare except for a table at one end, a cupboard at the other, and a Swiss cuckoo-clock on the wall that groaned unceasingly, as if to indicate that all these tropical rains and incantations were more than its stolid Calvinistic frame could endure.

The half-dozen lady candidates of the group smiled shyly at me, bobbing their heads up and down like inquiring flowers. Feminine initiates were in the minority however. The rest, more than a score, were men. All stood with bowed heads as one of the guides opened the proceedings by chanting a prayer, invoking the grace of Allah. He sounded like a muezzin calling the faithful to prayer from the snow-white minaret of an Arab mosque.

The second guide then took over and began to pace up and down between the silent ranks, pronouncing ethical exhortations, counselling one man to devote less time to gambling, and another not to think so much of carnal love. Evidently he could see into their hearts. The more advanced guides, whispered Mr. Sardjono, can also see what point the soul has reached in its ascension from the lowest plexus (or *chakram*, as they call them in accordance with Hindu terminology) at the level of the genital organs, to the *betal makmur* or plexus at the crown of the head, when perfect harmony is attained. After the second initiation, the soul is said to rise gradually, exercise by exercise, to the level of the heart plexus.

The initiates now took the vow—in Arabic—to worship God, and only one God (I was interested to observe that although they make use of this Muslim formula, they do not add the orthodox corollary: 'and his only Prophet Mohammed', since Sumarah recognizes all of the major prophets. Perhaps it would be truer to say that Sumarah is not so much concerned with prophet mediums as with the God-Presence, realized through direct communion).

★   ★   ★   ★

I had already remarked certain physical phenomena during the exercises of the 'ladies only' group, but these were much more conspicuous during the men's meditations. They assumed different forms, but the 'symptoms' remained fairly constant for each individual. The more advanced they were the quicker did they seem to reach the trance state when these physical phenomena manifested themselves. Sometimes it would be a slight swaying of the body, followed by a complete turn; other members adopted acrobatic postures, such as bending slowly backwards until their head nearly touched the floor; at times, they would change their position and walk over to the opposite side of the room. Very often one of the group would feel impelled to approach another Sumarah member and touch him lightly on the arm, remaining close to him for several minutes before returning to his original stance. This is said to be part of 'a purification process' during which a more detached individual unconsciously feels the moment when his colleages' minds begin to wander and need to be led back to a state of concentration. There is of course nothing unusual about such features for, as Fr. Thurston observes in his *Physical Phenomena of Mysticism*: 'Some people seem easily to pass into a state of ecstasy which bears an extremely close resemblance to the trance induced by hypnosis and—as occasionally happens in the hypnotic trance—they acquire strange powers, notably of clairvoyance and sometimes of telekinesis.'

The modern tendency in monastic and conventual communities of the West is to discourage all such abnormal, mystical inclinations during the discipline of noviceship and to put aspirants on guard against the development of singularities; likewise, although 'body movements' are taken as a matter of course by trance-loving Javanese, members of Sumarah are specifically warned against the dangers of occult powers and the striving after paranormal gifts. They are expressly forbidden to practise black magic and the guides inform every aspirant that if he or she is in possession of occult talents there is every likelihood that these will vanish once they have been initiated into Sumarah. I spoke with one second-grade initiation guide who had practised black magic for years before he reformed and asked to be allowed to join Sumarah. Not only did his clairvoyance leave him almost immediately, but during his first collective meditations, the mercury which had been injected into him by local magicians (in accordance with their belief that this helps to make the subject invulnerable to physical dangers) ran down his back and poured from his body on to the floor, to the astonishment of those present. Many Sumarah members do eventually acquire clairvoyance or clairaudience, but of a wholly spiritual nature, completely unconcerned with worldly matters and confined to the progress of the soul. For example, they can tell from a distance when one or the other of their friends are being attacked by some malevolent creature from the underworld, or when the ubiquitous *Idyadril* is attempting to drag them into a finely-woven net of temptation.

Certainly none of the physical phenomena I observed during Sumarah meditations were comparable to the astonishing contortions recorded by the contemporaries of some outstanding Western mystics, who were often completely transformed during their ecstasies. The famous seventeenth-century Spanish nun, Maria de Agreda, for instance, 'became radiant of countenance when she was praying and lost her natural weight so that she appeared to be floating in the air. If a nun blew in her direction, her body swayed with their breath as a feather or a leaf.' Her fellow-nuns were so proud of her that they made a public spectacle of the phenomenon, 'blowing' Maria to the convent grille where all could see her and gasp with vulgar amazement. When this accidentally came to her ears, it is reported that 'she prayed for the cessation of these outward manifestations of God's favour and her petition was granted'. Then there was the strange case of Veronica Laperechi who was sometimes seen to grow considerably taller than at normal times during her ecstatic trance or to roll herself up like a hedgehog.

The Indian mystic Meher Baba has also described the extraordinary behaviour of 'God-possessed' individuals in present-day India, but Sumarah—which is typically Javanese in inspiration and therefore less inclined to exaggeration, frowns upon these dangerous manifestations on the borderline of sanity. They would assuredly agree with the wise words of Pope Pius Benedict XIV, who laid down that: 'The existence of heroic sanctity is not guaranteed by stigmata, levitations and other charismata, however remarkable, but only by a consistently virtuous conduct in the trials of daily life and by an adequate use of the opportunities which may present themselves of promoting the service and glory of God.'

The practise of *sujud* and the constant worship of God, such is the ideal of Sumarah. There is nothing exotic or exceptional about an objective which is just as agonizingly difficult to put into execution in the East as it is in the West, particularly for those who live outside the discipline of a religious community and who must continually cope and compromise with the rough and tumble of the world. On the whole, however, I think that it *is* easier to 'turn the eye of the mind inward, to form an artificial solitude, retired amidst a crowd, calm amidst distraction and wise amidst folly' (Isaac d'Israeli) in Java, especially in quiet Jogjakarta, than it is in the urbanized West.

*   *   *   *

The Second Sumarah Initiation, and After

My *betjak* boy simply and quite sincerely could not locate No. 2 Loggi Ketchil behind the market, where an advanced Sumarah class was due to meet at seven o'clock on my last evening in Jogjakarta. In exasperation, I finally climbed out, left him, and stumbled up the dark, lonely street peering at the sullen houses with invisible numbers. The *betjak* boy, abashed and apologetic, followed a little way behind, on foot, from time to time urging me gently to climb back into his trishaw, for he was confident that he would ultimately find the right place—some time, somehow. At long last, however, I came upon the elusive No. 2. It turned out to be an infant school, consisting of a bare classroom with a weary smell of dried ink and chalk-filled dusters. A row of wooden chairs beside the blackboard at the top were already prepared to receive the founder, Mr. Sukino, the president, Dr. Surono Prodjohusodo, the secretary, Mr. Sardjono, Prince Prabuningrat (one of whose brothers was a member of Sumarah), and myself. Behind the chairs was a long desk at which Mrs. Sujitno and several of the male reporter-members were adjusting their copybooks and fountain-pens, for it is customary to transcribe the proceedings and the counsels given by Mr. Sukino in his trances. These go on uninterruptedly for hours, as I was shortly to discover; by 2 a.m. I was full of admiration for the stoic clerks who seemed to be magically immune from writer's cramp!

I met the Prince on the doorstep. He was on foot, although he was leading his bicycle, for he too had had difficulty in locating the humble schoolhouse. Mr. Sardjono came forward to relieve the Prince of his transport, which was whisked away by a youthful attendant into the darkness at the end of a corridor and to escort us to our place of honour, where we sat facing the hall, slightly embarrassed to be so exalted in the presence of the fraternity's 'star' members, who now began to trickle in leisurely and occupy the seats where infants huddled together in the daytime.

There were about sixty people in this gathering, of all types and ages. They sauntered in easily, exchanged greetings and cigarettes with their friends as if they had been meeting at a social club. Such equanimity and complete absence of neurotic tension is in my view the most convincing proof of the fraternity's healthy quality and sincerity of purpose. I mention cigarettes—an unmystical element in a gathering of this nature—because their use is characteristic of the humanized nature of this society. Unlike so many Indian sages who adhere to the medieval lust for self-mortification, Mr. Sukino does not believe that such extremes are helpful; when from time to time members ask him whether he would advise them to fast, stand on their heads, or refrain from touching women, Mr. Sukino shrugs his shoulders and tells them that if they feel such self-torture is a necessary means to their purification, well, it is up to them to try it out for themselves and see what good it does them. In his opinion, however (and here he approaches Buddhist tenets) nothing should be forced. Physical adjustments will take place naturally as the soul progresses, without a sudden, premature infliction of bodily penalties. *Sujud* . . . surrender. In God's time, when our hearts are ready to receive Him, He will come. Truly it has been said that the heart is the temple of the Holy Spirit. *Sujud* . . . how relaxed and free from strain everyone appeared to be! I looked at them closely, positive that I had passed many of them in Malioboro, never suspecting the secret of their inner life and the curious twist of fate that would bring me to this assembly. Two or three of the younger men were more intense than the rest; they did not amble amiably from desk to desk to pass a *kretek* to their friends, but buried their head in their arms and were soon lost in trance.

A birdlike murmur from behind a partition in the rear, accompanied by the occasional cry of a plaintive babe whose mother belonged to Sumarah, but whom Islam kept separated from the menfolk, revealed the presence of lady members. I peeped at them later and found them squatting comfortably on bamboo mats with a tea kettle well to the fore. It was they who provided refreshments during the interval. Some of them were only 'Sumarah wives' but the majority were active members of the fraternity.

Mr. Sukino joined us so unobtrusively that we did not even realize he had come until Mr. Sardjono suddenly exclaimed: 'Why, there he is!' and bowed smilingly to a gentleman who had seated himself at one of the desks in the body of the hall and was engaged in animated conversation with his elderly neighbour. I asked to be introduced and we walked over to shake hands with Sumarah's founder. I was very favourably impressed by the unaffected simplicity and humility of the man. How different from the arrogant, so-called 'Masters' of certain Oriental groups who demand absolute subjection from their disciples and surround themselves with an aura of self-assumed sanctity! There was nothing to distinguish Mr. Sukino outwardly from any other Sumarah member. He is broad and tall for a Javanese, almost as light-skinned as a Westerner, with keen, intensely kind eyes and a mobile, sensitive face. There was not the slightest trace of superiority in his bearing. Mr. Sardjono acted as my interpreter as I put question after question to him. Mr. Sukino answered them good-humouredly, smiling when—as he remarked—my queries betrayed too 'intellectual' an approach to such abstract matters and a Western impatience to want to grasp everything at once.

A few minutes later he sauntered up to his presidential chair at the end of the hall. Mrs. Sujitno wielded her authoritative gavel, the roll was efficiently called and then everybody lapsed into a meditative silence. One of the men in front of me began to jerk his head, and others swayed rhythmically to and fro. Mr. Sukino closed his eyes and remained immobile until inspiration began to pour through him; then he started to chant in a piercing voice, not unlike a *dalang's*, that penetrated into one's inner consciousness. His audience listened in a state of rapturous hypnosis, mentally limp but spiritually alert. Mr. Sukino opened his eyes after a while and appeared to be in a perfectly normal state; he was improvising a rhymed sermon in a language—so I was informed during the interval—that combined old Javanese words with expressions peculiar to Mr. Sukino himself. With the exception of one break for a glass of tea, the session went on continuously, without the slightest faltering or suggestion of fatigue.

The gist of what he said was translated for me afterwards by the indefatigable and devoted Mr. Sardjono and his wife. Although I could not understand at the time, I was not wearied by the rise and fall of the leader's voice. At the beginning, I was terrified lest it should have a sedative effect upon me, and I should fall asleep facing the audience; much to my surprise, however, the uncomprehended words had a fortifying effect; this must have been due to the close proximity of a being who radiates great spiritual power.

Here are a few extracts from Mr. Sukino's rhymed sermon. The curious will find nothing highly original about these phrases but they must remember that their purpose was entirely pragmatic; they were never intended to serve as examples of Javanese oratory. Furthermore, I have had to rely upon a translator whose knowledge of the English language and its vocabulary is somewhat limited:

'To be able to resist temptation, you must take refuge in God; you must remain tranquil and unruffled. Do not grieve over your shortcomings or your inability to understand all things clearly. Rely upon God with all your heart.

'Be truthful and simple in the meditations of your heart. Do not allow your mind to wander. If you do, your mind and heart will not be at prayer, you will stumble and fall into many pitfalls because of the lack of harmony between your body and soul.

'If you are not wholehearted in your determination to be a servant of God, if you are still in doubt, your lack of single-mindedness will result in painful mental confusion.

'Many so-called prophets and spiritual leaders, through lack of vigilance, have strayed from the right path. Riches and worldly honours began to attract them and they ceased to be honest. Durna, the ascetic (a *wayang* character) is an example of this type of individual; originally an authority on the inner life, he became a politician, putting worldly greatness above all else and in so doing he lost his holiness.

'People of this nature take pleasure in counting their riches and watching them increase. Those that seek after truth have to face many temptations; some of them degenerate and become mere profit-seekers, selling their teachings and mantrams for gain.

'May this serve to remind you of the dangers that confront you. Many apparently great men are in reality great deceivers—such practices are very common in our day and age.

'Above all, you need to cultivate harmony, silence, constant meditation upon God, and detachment from worldly cares.

'Pray increasingly—deep down in your heart. Do this day and night and whenever you have any spare time. Earning your living is a necessity which you must not neglect in your daily life, so always give of your best in your work.

'Do not be in a hurry. Practise your exercises slowly, but constantly. There must be peace in your heart.

'Be kind in thought, word, and deed. Be tolerant.

'A feeling of inner peace and joy is the sign that your prayers are being performed as they should be.

'Whether you succeed or not (spiritually) depends entirely upon yourself. Be earnest, because there are great dangers on the way.

'Sukino is only a medium through whom humanity must be awakened so that it will take refuge in God.

'It is not possible to attain spirituality through the sphere of thought; the intellect is not the medium for this. A brilliant brain does not ensure an entry into the world of the spirit.

'In Sumarah, dogmas, sacred books, mantrams, discursive prayers, are considered superfluous. Only two things are necessary: to serve God and to pray in your innermost heart.

'Although such practices are important, do not dwell upon whether or not you are making progress. Do not pause on the way. Never doubt or look back. God is with you until the end.

'When the "great feeling" begins to develop within you, charity will likewise begin to manifest itself—you will then think of others as yourself.

'There are today many religions, many schools of mysticism and occultism. Most people are fanatical about their creeds and doctrines, believing that only theirs is true. They ignore truth itself. . . .'

Mr. Sukino is a modern Indonesian patriot as well as a mystical leader. Mysticism and nationalism have often gone hand in hand in this country and a part of that night's sermon was concerned with highly practical matters, as the following remarks show:

'You must widen the sphere of your knowledge, especially in technology. This is very important if you want your country to rank as an equal with other nations.

'Knowledge is necessary, for it is the key to the hidden wealth of the world which will make your nation prosperous.

'Help to promote education so that your country may reach international status, but in doing this do not neglect the life of the spirit.'

*   *   *   *

During the tea break, which occurred when Mr. Sukino suddenly paused and reached out to the table in front of him for a glass of water to moisten his lips, everybody reverted instantly to their normal condition; some lit a cigarette and walked up and down to loosen their limbs, while others went out for a breath of air, because the atmosphere indoors, where all the windows had been closed against prying eyes, was stifling.

Mr. Sukino smiled and chatted affably with several Sumarah members; a medical student who spoke a little English came up to satisfy his curiosity about me; we ended by interviewing each other, for I wanted to find out many things about him and in particular whether many more of the young, scientifically trained generation felt the same need for Sumarah. The student replied that he could only answer for his faculty and that as far as he knew twenty of his fellow-students belonged to Sumarah because, he explained, it gives them, as well as all the others present that night—civil servants, garage hands, teachers, and market-vendors —a motive power in life, the spiritual drive behind the human machine without which existence would seem to be pointless.

After the interval came one of the 'collective checks' I referred to earlier. A slip of paper was passed to Mr. Sukino, which he read aloud, withholding the signature. This was a pathetic inquiry from one of the members who declared that he had heard a voice in a dream which he thought was the Voice of God; he had not been able to sleep at all since this shattering event. Would Mr. Sukino and the rest of the class confirm the authenticity of his revelation? Mr. Sukino now enjoined upon the assembly one of those 'quiet moments' so frequently resorted to by members of Moral Rearmament. This was followed by a brief consultation before Mr. Sukino pronounced the crushing verdict. The answer was an emphatic: 'No.' The man who thought he had heard the Voice of the Almighty was yet another of the many victims of self-delusion.

*   *   *   *

There was a mundane rush for bicycles when the meeting broke up at half-past two in the morning and the members dispersed to their respective beds and bamboo mats. A weary Mr. Sardjono trudged beside me in search of a *betjak*; we ultimately found a group of them converged together in wheel formation by the market-place. Their drivers, who were evidently homeless, sprawled across the seats, fast asleep. Eventually one of them stirred, rested his heavy eyes thoughtfully upon our faces, and agreed to drive me back to the hotel. Mr. Sardjono accompanied me, too tired to talk. (He had been one of those busily engaged in transcribing the six-hour sermon.)

The night was nearly over and so was my stay in Java. Four hours later I would be in the train bound for Djakarta and its airport. I felt closer to the Javanese now than I had ever been. I hoped that this sentiment was mutual and that it would endure, in the same way that I hope this story—which is now ending—will bring the Javanese, their grace, their inner strivings, and their quiet charm, nearer to you.

SUMARAH VOWS

1. The members of the Sumarah fraternity are convinced of the existence of God Who has created Heaven and Earth with all that is in them; they also acknowledge the existence of the Prophets and their Holy Books.

2. They vow to think of God at all times, to refrain from idolizing their ego (the 'I', the lower self), to rely upon truth, and to seek after contact with God (*sujud*) leading to 'self-surrender' to Him.

3. They shall make every effort to attain bodily health, inner peace, and the purification of the soul; they will also make every effort to ennoble their character, their thoughts, words, and deeds.

4. They shall make every endeavour to promote brotherhood founded upon deeply rooted love.

5. They will make every effort to widen their daily duties, not to ignore the needs of social life, to perform their duties to their nation, in order to promote order and peace in the world.

6. They vow to submit to the laws of their country, to respect their fellow-men, not to defame another man's creed; it is their duty to try with love to make it clear to all sects, all seekers of inner peace, and all religions that they should unite in their aspirations.

7. They shall refrain from evil, such as hurting and hating one another; every one of their actions should be unpretentious and true, performed patiently and accurately, without haste, without strain.

8. They shall do their best to widen their knowledge of world affairs as well as of the essence of things.

9. They will not be fanatical but rely upon truth, for the improvement of life in their community.

FOLK TALES OF CENTRAL ASIA

A collection of stories selected entirely from the oral tradition: from servants and royal courts, from teahouses and caravanserais — some of them just ahead of the industrial development which helps to wipe out such delightful examples of the treasures of human culture.

Amina Shah, who was brought up both in the East and West, has written and broadcast extensively on Eastern traditional lore.

'The specialists record, the results are printed and arrive in libraries, but the authentic magic is in the telling, when a spellbinder like Amina Shah takes wing.'

Doris Lessing in The Guardian

'Written down for enjoyment, not amassed as culture fodder.'

Times Literary Supplement

'Full of marvellous imagery.' *The Field*

FOLK TALES OF CENTRAL ASIA
by Amina Shah
The Octagon Press, £1.50 net.

DESTINATION MECCA

An exciting book of travel and exploration. Idries Shah lived in Saudi Arabia as the King's guest. Here he visits rulers, peasants, a guerrilla chief, bedouins, magicians and mystics.

'Intensely interesting.'

The Spectator

'As exciting as a good novel.'

Time Literary Supplement

'An unusual mixture of a travelogue and philosophy.'

Books and Bookmen

DESTINATION MECCA
By Idries Shah
The Octagon Press, 1971
£2.25 (hardback only) (Illustrated)

THE ELEPHANT IN THE DARK

'The Elephant in the Dark' deals with the interplay of Christianity and Islam and the Sufi conception of surrender to God. The materials originate in Idries Shah's work as a Visiting Professor at Geneva University (Switzerland), 1972/73.

'Between the lines in Elephant in the Dark (the title comes from an old Sufi fable about blindmen who reported on bits of an elephant they could not understand) Shah seems to suggest that the time is ripe for true ecumenism . . . might well be a third force that could transform a very sick world.'

Evening News

THE ELEPHANT IN THE DARK
By Idries Shah
The Octagon Press, 1974
£1.50 (hardback only)

AMONG THE DERVISHES

No ordinary book of travel, *Among the Dervishes* takes the reader into monasteries where ancient lore is still taught along the pilgrim road to forbidden Mecca, into the heart and mind of Asia.

Speaking several Oriental languages, travelling as a dervish pilgrim, O. M. Burke has lived and studied with ancient communities in the Near and Middle East — and this is the first-hand report.

.... "knowledgeable, realistic and unsentimental. Mr. Burke's book opens horizons that cause the mind to soar."

Sunday Telegraph

"This is the record of a remarkable journey . . . not one accessible to the academic scholar, or the idly curious, and this book is invaluable and in various ways."

Books and Bookmen

AMONG THE DERVISHES
by O. M. Burke
The Octagon Press, 1973
£3.00 net. (hardback) £1.75 net. (paperback)

SADI: THE ROSE GARDEN

Sadi's *Gulistan,* the Rose-Garden, is both one of the best-known of the Sufi classics and a major work of Persian literature.

SADI: THE ROSE GARDEN
Translated by E.B. Eastwick, C.B., M.A., F.R.S., M.R.A.S.
The Octagon Press, 1974
£3.50 (hardback) £2.00 (paperback)

TEACHINGS OF RUMI:

THE MASNAVI

Jalaluddin Rumi's great work, *The Masnavi*, was 43 years in the writing. During the past seven hundred years, this book, called by the Iranians 'The Koran in Persian,' a tribute paid to no other book, has occupied a central place in Sufism.

'*The Masnavi* is full of profound mysteries, and a most important book in the study of Sufism — mysteries which must, for the most part, be left to the discernment of the reader.'

F. Hadland Davis

'To the Sufi, if not to anyone else, this book speaks from a different dimension, yet a dimension which is in a way within his deepest self.'

Idries Shah

'The greatest mystical poet of any age.'

Professor R. A. Nicolson

'It can well be argued that he is the supreme mystical poet of all mankind.'

Professor A. J. Arberry

TEACHINGS OF RUMI: The Masnavi
Abridged and translated by E. H. Whinfield.
The Octagon Press, 1974
£4.00 net (hardback) £3.00 net (softback)

THE SPIRIT OF THE EAST

Today the kinship of all religious thought and dogma is becoming more apparent to mankind — and the value of Oriental thought to the Occidental mind is obvious. Here is a selection from Moslem, Parsee, Hindu, Hebrew, Confucian and other sources, chosen not only for their spiritual worth but also for the particular virtues of each creed which they represent.

The aim of this book is to introduce readers to the religious thought of the East, which — for reasons of language and other difficulties — they might otherwise have considered inaccessible.

". . . a wistful attempt towards showing a way of reconciling warring humanity by the circumvention of political ideology in favour of what could unite us . . . this book makes one dream of what now seem remote possibilities."
". . . as contemporary as a textbook on psychology."

Jewish Chronicle Literary Supplement

THE SPIRIT OF THE EAST
Sirdar Ikbal Ali Shah
The Octagon Press, 1974
£3.50 net. (hardback) £1.75 net. (paperback)

ORIENTAL MYTICISM

Professor E. H. Palmer's systematisation of these Sufi materials has been regarded as essential reading in its subject for many years.

ORIENTAL MYTICISM
By Professor E.H. Palmer
The Octagon Press, 1974
£2.00 (hardback) £1.00 (paperback)